JUDGING THE JUDGES

JUDGING THE JUDGES

K. MAHESH

BISHWAJIT BHATTACHARYYA

GYAN PUBLISHING HOUSE

NEW DELHI-110002

JUDGING THE JUDGES

(Law, Police, Politics, Media, Sociology)

ISBN : 81-212-0606-5

Published in 1999 in India by
Gyan Publishing House
5, Ansari Road
New Delhi 110 002
Laser Typesetting: Grow Computers, Delhi.
Printed at Mehra Offset Press, New Delhi.

CONTENTS

EDITORS' NOTE

The Indian judiciary has recently acquired the distinction of being a revered, respected, feared and, paradoxically, the most criticised wing of the State.

Revered because of its sterling role in protecting fundamental rights of individuals, cutting across nationality, caste, creed or religion. Respected because of its fierce independence while purging corruption amongst high public functionaries. And criticised by these very functionaries for having been exposed by the judiciary. Housing scam, fodder scam, to name a few, have been exposed only by the judiciary.

It is hardly surprising, therefore, that cries of curbing 'judicial activism' keep surfacing from the executive and the legislature periodically. A section of the executive and the legislature, in collusion with undesirable elements, have for long played havoc with the Indian polity. The Vohra Committee report on the nexus between criminals and executive makes distressful reading. Amidst this dismal situation the role of the Indian judiciary remained somewhat muted and subdued till 1993.

1993 marked the watershed year in the history of Indian jurisprudence with the pronouncement of the judgement of the Supreme Court Advocates-on-Record Association case (AIR 1994 SC 268). This judgement snatched away from the executive the power of appointment, posting and transfer of judges and vested the same on the judiciary itself. The judiciary hereafter started asserting its true role and firmly put the executive and the legislature within constitutional bounds. Public interest litigation became more pronounced. Judicial fiat touched almost every facet of public life; the executive and the legislature had to bow down before the judiciary time and again. Thus, the Indian judiciary became truly independent after almost 45 years of political independence. The special reference made to the Supreme Court by the President of India on 23.7.98 in exercise of his powers conferred under Article 143 (1) of the Constitution of India resulted only in reaffirmation of the supremacy of the judiciary subject to the condition that the Chief Justice of India is obliged to comply with the norms and requirement of the consultation process with his senior colleagues.

But, then, the true independence of the judiciary and judicial activism threw open a far graver controversy; the power struggle between the judiciary on one hand and the legislature and the executive on the other became intense. As a natural corollary, the performance of the judiciary came under closer scrutiny. It is in this context that the topic of judging the judges gained importance, particularly against the background that the impeachment procedure to remove errant judges as enshrined in the Constitution has virtually failed.

Judging the performance of the judiciary has today become a fashionable topic, particularly amongst the legislature and the executive. The idea is obviously to curb the expanding horizon of judicial intervention, and even perhaps to browbeat the judiciary. To the non-litigant the judiciary is a symbol of idealism and hope. The litigant, however, is not much impressed! How many years, nay decades, a case will take to get decided and how much of misfortune he may have to encounter in the process is anybody's guess. Misfortune may well turn the litigant into a pauper after paying fees to lawyers. And to crown it all, in the end the court judgement may well be contrary to his bonafide perception, legal advice and Article 141 of the Constitution of India, which stipulates that the law declared by the Supreme Court shall be binding on all the courts within the territory of India. The uncertainty about law and court judgements was compounded with the decision of Bengal Immunity Company Limited Vs. State of Bihar (AIR 1955 SC 661) in which the Supreme Court interpreted Article 141 to mean that it does not include Supreme Court itself. Which means the law declared by the Supreme Court is not binding on itself. Add to this the common law doctrine of Stare Decisis which is different from the broad doctrine of precedent prevalent in all developed systems in that if certain conditions are fulfilled, an English Judge has either to follow the previous decision or else to distinguish it. In 1955 the House of Lords held that its decisions were absolutely binding on itself (London Street Tramways Limited Vs. London Country Council (1898) A.C. 375). But in India, as in the USA, the Supreme Court has freely exercised the right to reconsider its own decision. In this connection, it is interesting to note the dissenting judgement of Justice Hegde in the case ITO Vs. T.S.D. Nadar (AIR 1968 SC 623) where he observed that :

> "...the decision of this Court should not be overruled excepting under compelling circumstances...Every time this Court overrules its previous decision, the confidence of the public in the soundness of the decision of this Court is bound to be shaken...in law finality is of utmost importance...".

These imply that even after having been armed with a settled case law, the litigant may still find the law being yet again unsettled.

All these grim realities in the shape of uncertainties, delays and mounting costs may progressively alienate bonafide litigants from the judiciary. Should that actually happen, a death knell will be sounded to the rule of law in India. This must be prevented at all cost.

What can be done to prevent this? Listen to the criticism against the judiciary with a receptive mind and initiate measures to rectify the aberrations. That is the idea of this book. In a democracy like India, criticism against any wing of the State is a healthy phenomenon so long as this acts as a beacon light for those who are being criticised.

Apart from the criticism on account of the chronic backlog of cases, today's criticism against the judiciary primarily springs from power struggle. The executive and the legislature are unable to accept the fact that the founding fathers of the Constitution had placed supreme trust in the wisdom of the judiciary. In fact, the ding-dong battle between the judiciary and the legislature has been going on in India since the Golaknath decision (AIR 1967 SC 1643), followed by Kesavananda Bharati (AIR 1973 SC 1461) decision of the Supreme Court. Whether the Parliament is or the Supreme Court is supreme has still not been entirely free from controversy. The Supreme Court has knocked down constitutional amendments carried out by the Parliament on the ground of their being violative of the basic structure doctrine, and therefore ultravires of the amending powers of the Parliament. Likewise, the Supreme Court's decisions too have been nullified by the Parliament. One cannot forget how the Muslim divorced women's legislation was enacted by the Parliament only to nullify a decision of the Supreme Court. Even Article 329 (4) of the Constitution with regard to election of Speaker and Prime Minister was inserted by the Parliament in order to allow Mrs. Gandhi's appeal before the Supreme Court after being unseated by the Allahabad High Court which found her guilty of corrupt election practices and disqualifying her for six years. Of course, the Supreme Court reached its finest hour when it struck down the newly added Article 329 (4) in the landmark judgement of Indira Nehru Gandhi Vs. Raj Narain AIR 1975 SC 2299.

Not that there is anything radically wrong with such power struggle. This is an inevitable concomitant of any vibrant democracy. In fact, all the three wings of the State acting harmoniously with each other can possibly give rise to a worst form of state despotism! So, it may not always be in the best interest of democracy if all the wings of the State toe each other's lines. But as long as the Constitution gives powers to the judiciary alone to interpret the law, the other wings of the State must accept with grace the judiciary's superiority in this respect.

Which provision of law gives the edge to the judiciary over the Parliament? Article 245 of the Constitution stipulates that the Parliament's law-making power has been circumscribed by the provisions of the Constitution. And, ultimately, it is the Supreme Court that has the final say in adjudicating as to whether or not the provisions of the Constitution have been followed or circumvented. It is the interpretative power of the constitutional provisions that makes the Supreme Court the most powerful body among different organs of the State. Then, in terms of Article 142, the Supreme Court in exercise of its jurisdiction may pass such decree or make such order as is necessary for doing complete justice in any case or matter pending before it. It also empowers the Supreme Court to make any order for the purpose of securing the attendance of any person, the discovery or production of any documents, or the investigation or punishment of any contempt of itself. Although this power of the Supreme Court is subject to the provisions of any law made in this behalf by the Parliament, as already discussed, it is the Supreme Court that will ultimately decide whether the Parliament while enacting any legislation has transgressed any Constitutional provision.

Of course, there have been vaild criticism in some quarters that Article 142 cannot be used by the Supreme Court as a source of power. Nor does this article ipso-facto give any jurisdiction to the Supreme Court to entertain a petition. The words 'in exercise of jurisdiction' in the article clearly signify that this provision can be resorted to only if the Apex Court exercises its jurisdiction through another provision. Clearly, independent jurisdiction and source of power cannot be acquired through this provision. It is hoped that the Apex Court in due course will interpret this article in the true spirit which the founding fathers of the Constitution had intended and set at rest all controversies in this respect.

Then, in terms of Article 144 of the Constitution, all authorities, civil and judicial, in the territory of India, shall act in aid of the Supreme Court. And finally, Article 141 stipulates that the law declared by the Supreme Court shall be binding on all courts within the territory of India.

That, then, is the source and ambit of awesome powers of the Indian judiciary. With so much of power, it is but natural that there is all round expectation that the judiciary will exercise them judiciously, curb misdeeds of other wings of the State and will simultaneously set its own house in order. It is in response to such expectations that this book elicits views from a wide cross section of eminent jurists, judges, journalists, statesmen, parliamentarians, scholars, academicians and Civil Servants, past or present.

Amongst the notable authors who have contributed to this book, Mr. Ram Jethmalani, an eminent jurist, and a Union Cabinet Minister, favours the constitution of a National Judicial Commission to monitor judicial performance. Mr. Jethmalani regrets that in recent years there have been widely reported allegations of judicial misconduct and a disconcerting compromise of integrity and impartiality.

Justice H.R. Khanna, a former judge of the Supreme Court of India, argues that the judiciary should not try to take over the function of the executive even on a limited scale. He feels that of all the different types of despotism, the judicial despotism is most irrational, illogical and inexcusable. The judiciary, he argues, must remain beyond the purview of any political controversy and must not allow its image to be smeared. Justice Khanna laments non-conviction of criminals in major cases of murder, rape, extortion, culpable homicide etc. He also criticises the judiciary for resorting to contempt jurisdiction. According to Justice Khanna contempt of court is no answer to genuine criticism of courts.

Justice V.R. Krishna Iyer, the noted former judge of the Supreme Court of India, questions whether delinquencies of judges should be kept hidden for ever in the name of defending the integrity and credibility of the institution? He does not favour the power to pronounce a verdict on the judge to be vested in the bar. He regrets that currently in India there is no alternative procedure to ventilate genuine grievances against a judge. In his inimitable style the former judge says:

> "...their lordships in full panoply will still invite attack unless they become institutionally and individually accountable to the country and be punishable for unbecoming behaviour, dereliction of duty and common criminality."

Justice Krishna Iyer laments that judges sometimes commit contempt by intemperate tongue. In this context, the former judge advocates a code of conduct for dignified behaviour of judges. A bad judge, he says, with a wag's tongue or rude mood may do great harm to the institution. He suggests the constitution of a Judicial Performance Commission as advocated by David Pannick Q.C. (vide judges) with adaptation to Indian conditions. The former judge suggests that judges against whom allegations have been levelled must be cleared by their peers. He argues that judges are not the voice of infallibility and must, like other institutions of our Republic, submit to public scrutiny, invigilation by socially sensitive peers and be broadly accountable to the collective sovereign, the people of India.

Noted judge, Mr. Prem Kumar, in his learned exposition has highlighted the positive aspects of Public Interest Litigation (PIL). He concludes that what is being described as judicial activism is, in fact, judicial pragmatism and judicial statesmanship. The learned judge argues at great length to buttress the point that self-reliance is the foundation of independence of the judiciary and no price is too heavy to secure it. The judge also asserts that judges selected should be men of character and integrity.

Mr. V.N. Narayanan, Editor of the Hindustan Times criticises the contempt power exercised by courts in as much as the person who is prosecuting the contemnor is also the judge sentencing him (the contemnor). Mr. Narayanan also criticises irresponsible utterances from the bench made by the judges. He questions, can the judiciary remain a forbidden territory from public criticism? Mr. Narayanan argues that the law is sufficiently flexible and continues to be subjective and gets moulded according to the philosophy and temper of the judge(s) concerned. He highlights that there is a serious school of thought that the power of contempt for scandalising the Court needs to be legislatively circumscribed to remove the vague element of fear that prevails in the minds of public men, journalists, and commentators.

Mr. Sitaram Yechuri, a noted Marxist leader argues that judges, after all, are not infallible. He, therefore, advocates a system whereby fallibility of judges will be put under some kind of a check without necessarily questioning their integrity. He suggests constitution of National Judicial Commission, with appropriate amendments to the Constitution, for appointment of judges. Mr. Yechuri criticises the judiciary for transgressing its limits and entering into the domain of the executive and the legislature. Yet he concedes that there is a tremendous amount of faith that the common man has in the judiciary. This faith, he argues, ought to be sustained.

Mr. Syed Shahabuddin, former diplomat and a politician, argues that there is a need to decentralise and reform the judicial system. He criticises the mode of appointment to the higher judiciary which, he feels, is shrouded in mystery. He highlights that the procedure to impeach judges has proved to be so cumbersome, complicated and time-consuming that its efficacy as the instrument of control and accountability has been universally found to be non-existent. The implication, he notes with regret, is that in a de facto sense, in the High Court or the Supreme Court, a judge is not accountable, unless he breaks all the rules in the books! Mr. Shahabuddin, however, advocates financial independence of the judiciary. He also suggests constitution of Indian Judicial Service. Judiciary, he feels, should have an In-House Committee to probe allegations of nepotism, corruption, impropriety or misbehaviour.

Mr. R.K. Jain, the President of the Supreme Court Bar Association argues that the Second Judges Transfer case is palpably wrong and needs reconsideration by a larger bench. Mr. Jain argues that in no democracy elected representatives of the people have been kept out from the process of selecting the judges. He argues that the bar should be consulted before judges are appointed to the bench. This practice, Mr. Jain highlights, is followed in the USA. Shri Jain argues that dependence on the executive in financial matters interferes with the independence of judiciary. Shri Jain, therefore, advocates complete financial autonomy for the Supreme Court and the High Courts. He advocates an active judiciary and concludes that judicial activism is the need of the day.

Mr. P.P. Rao, former President of the Supreme Court Bar Association and a senior advocate, analyses the influence of the media in judging the judges. He argues that special privilege to the press is a time-worn fallacy, and sooner the misconception that the press is not accountable to the law is removed the better it will be. He feels that no editor has a right to assume the role of investigator or try to prejudice the court against any person. Mr. Rao argues that media coverage should not be allowed unwittingly to facilitate media intrusion in administration of justice. He points out that after the advent of electronic media, the tendency to render populistic judgements or pass orders which would hit the headlines is, regrettably, on the increase.

Shri Hardev Singh, Senior Advocate, argues that judges should have unblemished character and judicial rectitude, apart from maintaining uprightness, integrity. He too advocates constitution of National Judicial Commission to keep a check on the judiciary, since, according to him, higher judiciary is not accountable in our constitutional scheme.

Dr. Abhishek Singhvi, former Additional Solicitor General, and a Senior Advocate, emphasises the need to bring about transparency in judicial appointments and to ensure judicial accountability. Disciplining errant judges is another factor that Dr. Singhvi has stressed.

Mr. K.T.S. Tulsi, former Additional Solicitor General, and a Senior Advocate, dwells at length upon the criminal justice system in India and laments that the convinction rate in criminal trials in India is perhaps one of the lowest in the world, about 6.4 per cent. Accordingly, Mr. Tulsi argues, conviction has ceased to be a deterrent for the offenders. The twin problems of criminal justice system in India, according to Mr. Tulsi, is that it has become completely insensitive to the victim as well as to the witness.

Dr. Surat Singh, and advocate of the Supreme Court, highlights how the judiciary failed the people of India during emergency. Dr. Singh extensively argues to prove the point that the Indian Supreme Court in the post 1993 phase has invariably corrected the mistakes of the executive and the legislative wings of the government to act as protector of fundamental values of the Indian society.

Professor Aswini K. Ray, a noted academician from JNU, regrets that it is the parallel system of 'justice', along with the parallel economy, which is increasingly becoming the dominant component of the citizens' conflict-resolution and grievance-redressal mechanism. In this sense, says Professor Ray, by default the judicial system has become dialectically linked with the criminalised system of governance in modern India's anomic politics. According to him, criticism against the judiciary cannot be allowed to be stifled on the plea of the "independence of the judiciary". Professor Ray feels that like most other democratic institutions of modern India , whatever one generalises, the contrary is also true. This duality between the operational and the dysfunctional, which characterises all Indian institutions is most damaging for the judicial system, argues Professor Ray. He concludes that adjudication becomes perverse oppression when exercised by individuals with questionable credentials within an institutional system with weak popular legitimacy.

Ms. Puja Khattar, a noted scholar, critically analyses evolution of concept of social justice and judicial activism. She lauds the creative role played by the Indian judiciary in this respect. She recalls that as early as 1957 when he joined the Supreme Court, Justice Gajendragadkar may be said to have delivered the first of a series of blows on behalf of social justice. Ms. Khattar emphasises that it is up to the legal profession more than any other section of society to quicken the pace of socio-economic change. She concludes that in a democratic country committed to the task of establishing socio-economic equality, the centre of gravity of law lies not so much on the legislature, court-rooms or chamber of jurists, but in the unsatisfied but legitimate hopes and aspirations of the common citizens of the country.

Mr. K.P.S. Gill, the former Director General of Police of Punjab highlights the inadequacies of the judiciary. He laments that the convinction rate in criminal cases as it stands today is below six-and-a-half per cent. Mr. Gill criticises the Second Judges' Transfer Case and goes on to argue that India is the only country in the world where judges select themselves, determine their own transfers and discipline themselves. He concludes by recommending setting up an independent Judicial Commission which would be responsible, not only for appointments and transfers, but also to see to it that judges perform their duties in keeping with the high traditions of the legal profession and the judiciary.

Mr. Joginder Singh, former Director of CBI, highlights that the border line between the contempt of court and criticism of court is very thin. Crossing this line can have dangerous consequences since in such a proceeding the judge acts in dual capacity both as a judge and a prosecutor. Mr. Singh also questions the capacity of the judiciary (in terms of infrastructure, manpower and equipment) to handle the workload it is required to do. He quotes some interesting statistics to prove his point that the situation is slowly slipping out.

Mr. R.K. Takkar, a former Secretary to the Government of India, recalls some of his personal encounters with the judiciary during his long tenure with the Indian Administrative Service. Shri Takkar finds little justification for a practice where a Secretary to the Government of India is hauled up for contempt arising out of the act of his subordinates. He advocates complainants of false criminal complaints (to settle personal scores) to be sent to jail by magistrates. Mr. Takkar also squarely blames public servants for large pendency in courts in service matters. He advocates out of court settlement in most such cases.

Mr. N.K. Singh, a former Joint Director of CBI, commences with the argument that the judiciary has failed us. He quotes specific examples to substantiate his point. Mr. Singh criticises courts for liberally granting anticipatory bails to notorious criminals whose activities have global ramifications. He also reveals as to how he was abruptly transferred while handling a sensitive case, and how the judiciary did not come to his rescue. Mr. Singh, however, concedes that recent judicial activism has come as a welcome relief.

Mr. H.S. Sandhu, a serving officer of the Indian Police service, highlights new dimensions of police accountability vis-a-vis judicial activism and argues that the police force in the country is overworked and in trying to please all its masters, it could not satisfy any of them. Mr. Sandhu argues that in the recent past cabinet ministers have shown a tendency to shift the responsibility to the courts for matters which the government is too weak to decide for itself, with the result that the judiciary is being caught in a political web. Mr. Sandhu feels that a High Court's order asking a Joint Director of the CBI not to report to his boss is taking judicial activism too far. According to him, too much of judicial activism could erode the credibility of courts, imperil the rule of law and lead to lawlessness. He concludes that police cannot be controlled by external agencies.

Needless to mention, the papers in this volume reflect the views of the individual authors.

It is the fond hope of the Editors that the readers will appreciate the judiciary's role, which has been noticed from different perspectives by a number of eminent and knowledgeable authors. The judiciary requires to trim itself and move faster to maintain its pre-eminent position.

New Delhi, India **K. Mahesh**

Dec 26, 1998 **Bishwajit Bhattacharyya**

LIST OF CONTRIBUTORS

1. **Ram Jethmalani** — Union Minister for Urban Affairs & Employment and an eminent jurist
2. **H.R. Khanna** — Former Judge of the Supreme Court of India
3. **V.R. Krishna Iyer** — Former Judge of the Supreme Court of India
4. **V.R. Krishna Iyer** — Former Judge of the Supreme Court of India
5. **Prem Kumar** — Secretary, Press Council of India and former Chief Metropolitan Magistrate, New Delhi
6. **V.N. Narayanan** — Editor, The Hindustan Times
7. **Sitaram Yechuri** — A noted Marxist Leader
8. **Syed Shahabuddin** — A former Diplomat and a Politician
9. **R.K. Jain** — President of the Supreme Court Bar Association and a Senior Advocate, Supreme Court of India
10. **P.P. Rao** — Senior Advocate, Supreme Court of India and a former President of the Supreme Court Bar Association
11. **Hardev Singh** — Senior Advocate, Supreme Court of India

12. **Dr. Abhishek Manu Singhvi**	Vice President, Supreme Court Bar Association and a Senior Advocate, Supreme Court of India
13. **K.T.S. Tulsi**	Former Additional Solicitor General of India and a Senior Advocate, Supreme Court of India.
14. **Dr. Surat Singh**	Advocate Supreme Court of India
15. **Prof. Aswini K. Ray**	A noted Academician from JNU
16. **Puja Khattar**	A Noted Scholar
17. **K.P.S. Gill**	Former Director General of Police, Punjab
18. **Joginder Singh**	Former Director, CBI
19. **R.K. Takkar**	Former Secretary, Govt. of India
20. **N.K. Singh**	Former Jt. Director, CBI
21. **H.S. Sandhu**	An I.P.S. Officer
22. **K. Mahesh**	Officer on Special Duty to the Union Minister for Urban Affairs & Employment

1

JUDGING THE JUDGES

Ram Jethmalani

The Greek philosopher Socrates (470-399 B.C.) described four qualifications for a judge: he should be able to hear courteously; answer wisely; consider soberly and decide impartially. Through the ages, it has been assumed that judges by and large live up to these qualifications. The belief has persisted despite credible evidence of serious deficiencies and deviations in individual cases.

The Indian Constitution created a Republic not merely a democracy. Our republican Constitution withdrew certain subjects from vicissitudes of political controversy and placed them beyond the reach of majorities and legislators. Equality of all, the freedom of conscience and religious belief and the liberty of speech and expression are conspicuous illustrations. Armed with such fantastic rights, it is the individual who is sovereign and the majority is under Constitutional shackles. Dignity and worth of human personality constitute the basic aim of our polity. Inevitably however my right to swing my arms must end at my neighbours nose.

The individual citizen is at every point of time under threat from the holders of political power, from insensitive and corrupt bureaucrats and from an insensitive police force. Perforce he turns to the courts for protection and security. The Constitution in turn conferred awesome powers on the judges, particularly the judges of the Supreme Court of India; with power to annul even an Act of Parliament as unconstitutional and void, and the power to enforce judgements and order by the power of punishing for contempt, the Court became the most powerful Court in the world. The honesty and integrity of the individual judge naturally became of pivotal importance to the individual and society in general.

It is trite that judges neither control the purse nor the sword. They neither have the army at their disposal nor access to the State treasury. In a show down with other branches of government, the judge is bound to be worsted, a calamity against which he can be immunised only by the confidence and faith of the people who can be expected to back him. The people alone can neutralise the arrogance of political power, and the venality of the bureaucrat. The price of the people's support is an impeccable character wholly above suspicion.

It is unfortunate that in recent years there have been widely reported allegations of judicial misconduct and a disconcerting compromise of integrity and impartiality. The judges as a family have registered no adequate response to this menacing development. Serious instances were brought to light not by any mechanisms forged by the judiciary itself but by courageous members of the bar generally supported by prestigious associations and Bar Councils. When Justice Ramaswamy of the Supreme Court came to be exposed by a member of the Bar and all his efforts to instal an investigation with the help of a pliant Attorney-General and despicable Law Minister came to naught, the Speaker of the Lok Sabha created a Committee of Judges mandated by Parliamentary Statute to investigate the charges. After a painstaking inquiry substantially all charges were held proved against the judge. Even so the thick-skinned judge refused to resign believing that he will successfully manipulate a corrupt political party and prevent a final vote of impeachment. He proved right. The Ruling Party deviously turned the controversy into a north-south controversy and by the simple device of not voting prevented a two-thirds majority vote required by the Constitution. The redeeming feature was that not one vote was cast in favour of the corrupt judge.

The frustration of the impeachment process by a corruption ridden political party has inevitably raised the question "who will judge the judges?" It is obvious that the executive who is the major litigant before the courts neither be trusted to select the judges nor can it have the power to remove them. This will be totally subversive of judicial independence. Even in the Gupta case of 1982, in which by its own decision the Supreme Court threw judicial independence to the winds and ruled in favour of the executive paramountcy. Justice P.N. Bhagwati was constrained to admit the need for change. This is what he said:

> We would rather suggest that there must be a collegium to make recommendation to the President in regard to appointment of a Supreme Court or High Court Judge. The recommending authority should be more broad-based and there should be consultation with wider interests. If the collegium is composed of persons who are expected to have knowledge of the persons who may be fit for appointment on the Bench and of qualities required for appointment and this last requirement is absolutely essential—it would go a long way towards securing the right kind of Judges, who would be truly independent in the sense we have indicated above and who would invest the judicial process with significance and meaning for the deprived and exploited sections of humanity. We may point out that even countries like Australia and New Zealand have veered round to the view that *there should be a Judicial Commission for appointment of the higher judiciary.*

Since then formidable public opinion has crystalised in favour of the proposal. This includes the powerful opinion of the Law Commission expressed in its 121st Report.

A Constitution Amendment Bill moved by me in 1990 is a model and all subsequent Bills of the same kind closely approximate to it. National Judicial Commission consisting of the Chief Justice of India, the Chairman of the Bar Council of India, the Lokpal, if any, the Leader of the Opposition in the House of the People and a distinguished academician having special knowledge of law and legal literature nominated by the President in his sole discretion (not on the advice of the Cabinet) will have the power to appoint, to remove and to transfer. The National Judicial Commission will monitor judicial performance at all times and evolve suitable procedures, consonant with natural justice and its own effectiveness.

Judges, nor can it have the power to remove them. This will be totally subversive of judicial independence. Even in the Gupta case of 1982, in which by its own decision the Supreme Court threw judicial independence to the winds and ruled in favour of the executive paramountcy, Justice P.N. Bhagwati was [illegible] the need for change. This is what he said:

> We would rather suggest that there must be a collegium to make recommendation to the President in regard to appointment of a Supreme Court or High Court Judge. The recommending authority should be more broad-based and there should be consultation with wider interests. If the collegium is composed of persons who are expected to have knowledge of the persons who may be fit for appointment on the Bench and of qualities required for appointment and this last requirement is absolutely essential—it would go a long way towards securing the right kind of Judges who would be truly independent in the sense we have indicated above and who would invest the judicial process with significance and meaning for the deprived and exploited sections of humanity. We may point out that even countries like Australia and New Zealand have veered round to the view that there should be a Judicial Commission for appointment of the Judges.

Since then, considerable public opinion has crystallised in favour of the proposal. This is also the powerful opinion of the Law Commission [illegible] Report.

A Constitution amendment Bill moved by me in 1990 is a model and all subsequent Bills of the same kind closely approximate to it. A National Judicial Commission consisting of the Chief Justice of India, the Chairman of the Bar Council of India, the Leader, if any, the Leader of the Opposition in the House of the People and a distinguished academician having special knowledge of law and legal literature nominated by the President in his sole discretion (not on the advice of the Cabinet) will have the power to appoint, to remove and to transfer. The National Judicial Commission will monitor judicial performance at all times and evolve suitable procedures, consonant with natural justice and its own effectiveness.

2

THE ROLE OF THE JUDICIARY

H.R. Khanna

So far the political bosses assumed that they were above the law. The Judiciary has ensured that howsoever high you may otherwise be, the law is above you and you cannot escape the infection of its provisions. As it is we find that it is the act of the Judiciary in making the investigating agencies perform the task assigned to them by the law that corruption, amassing wealth (by high public functionaries) have come to light and the political bosses who were working under a smug assumption that investigating agencies being under them could never do anything against them in the matter now are feeling scared. The second thing which I wish to emphasize is that Judges must not allow themselves to be seduced by quick charted temptation to take over the governance of the country. The governance of the country is a task assigned by the Constitution to the executive wing of the State. If judiciary actually tries to take over this task it may actually not only disrupt the constitutional balance, it may actually result in a disaster. Judiciary has neither expertise nor is it a proper body to take over the governance of the country. It has to be borne in mind that Judiciary is a non-elective body. There is no provision in our constitution as there is in the Japanese Constitution that Judges of the Apex Court must every nine years obtain the confidence of the electorate as to whether they are fit to hold the job or not. The Judiciary being a non-elective body cannot and should not try to dethrone the Executive and take over its functions even on a limited scale. The role of the Judiciary is akin to that of a trusted guardian of the Constitution to ensure that no one indulges in trangression of the provisions of the constitution. If other organs or wings of a state transgress the limits of their authority, one can always approach the courts to seek the redress. If the Judiciary itself by act of judicial despotism tries to take over and transgresses that limit would the aggrieved parties actually approach and seek the judicial redress? Of all the different types of despotism the judicial despotism, I submit is more irrational, illogical and inexcusable. Even if the Judiciary actually tries to take over the role of other wings of the State, it would be diluting the responsibility of the Executive and diverting the criticism regarding decisions taken and attract that criticism to itself. Judiciary must remain beyond the perview of any political controversies and must not allow its image to be smeared by any such thing. The main task of the Judiciary, I submit is to decide the cases that come up before them. Proper administration of Justice requires that cases must be disposed of without delay and in many cases we find that Justice delayed is as bad as Justice denied. It is in this context that I would like to tell you that during the early years of independence we saw to it that cases were disposed of as expeditiously as possible. I was the District and Sessions Judge of Ferozepur which had the largest number of murder cases in the country. I had three Additional District Judges but we ensured that every murder case was disposed of within a period of two months from the date of filing of the challan in the Court of the Committing Magistrate. The time taken during commitment was during recording of evidence before the committing magistrate. The commitment was ordered and then the trial in the Court of Sessions and the pronouncement of the judgement. The period should not exceed two months. If in any case the time taken for the disposal of the murder cases was more than two months, a report had to be sent justifying the circumstances as to what had actually led to the delay. It was my experience during my stay there that not even once during the period of four years was a murder case ever adjourned because of the non-presence of the witnesses. I remember, in 1955 we had floods all over and Ferozepur was cut off from the rest of the country. There was a double murder case which was coming up, a top lawyer, Miss C. Rai, had come from Chandigarh to conduct that case. There was her one witness which was living in a remote village which was absolutely cut off from Ferozepur. But the prosecution saw to it that witness too was present at the time of the hearing. He was brought on a bloated skin of a buffalo and he was actually present in the court at the time of the hearing and the case was not adjourned. So far as criminal cases in the court of Magistrates were concerned, those cases were disposed of within a period of four months. It would seldom happen that a witness coming to a court of law had to go back without the recording of his evidence. The magistrates had to make a report as to why a witness who was present, his evidence could not be recorded. Now things are entirely different. Witnesses come to courts of law, they wait there for hours together, days together and then they go back without their evidence been recorded. It is a very unhappy state of affairs. So far as civil cases are concerned it had to be ensured that a civil suit must be decided within a period of one year from the date of its filing. There were some heavy civil cases but then the subordinate Judges had to submit their report as to why the case had taken more than a year. That was the state of affairs. Now if you start a civil litigation it has the virtual effect of the feeding litigations to your descendants. It's a very unhappy situation. Who is responsible for this delay? We can certainly attribute this delay to the failure to appoint enough number of Judges to cope up with the heavy pendency. But the Judiciary also cannot shirk its responsibility in the matter of accumulation of all heavy backlog of cases. Both the Executive and the Judiciary are guilty in this respect. There's another thing to which I want to draw your attention and that is the non-conviction of criminals in major cases of murder, rape, extortion and culpable homicide. As it is, we find that in majority of cases the major culprits escape punishment for the crime committed by them. The criminal law is supposed to be the most potent instrument of self-defence. If major culprits are not punished then it causes disillusionment and loss of faith in the judiciary. The victims are the relatives of the victims, associates of the victims and in that case they resort to extra legal methods to settle score with the culprits and this leads to a chain of crimes. This means the effacement of the Rule of Law. We must not allow this to happen. The other thing which I want to emphasize is that every decision without some kind of precedent cannot be looked upon as an act of Judicial innovation. Judicial decisions have to be backed by well-reasoned arguments. You cannot say, no judge of the highest court can say, well look here I have given the decision that no constitutional law of land can challenge. There's a difference between an act of draftsmanship and a judicial fiat which is not backed by any kind of well-reasoned arguments. Judges have to ensure that the evolution of law has to be slow, smooth and by a process of going from one state to the other, otherwise it would give a jolt to the evolution of law and is not in keeping with the tradition of law which has to be inherited through all these years. Another disturbing trend which has come to the fore is the resort to proceedings for contempt of court. Judiciary has to earn reverence through the test of truth. Judiciary cannot seek reverence by resorting to the contempt of court. Contempt of court is no answer to genuine criticism of the courts. By resorting to contempt of court you cannot pressurise the criticism against the judiciary. The judges have to bear in mind that there are many occasions when the general feeling is that they have gone astray. General criticism of the court has to be accepted by the judiciary. In England, I was reading that the law reviews are now becoming the highest Court of appeal. In the House of Lords in England the language used regarding some of the judgements was very harsh and in India we are not accustomed to this thing. Judges would not take it in good sense. Very harsh terms were actually used but the judges accepted it and did not try to impose, did not try to proceed for contempt of court. I have said many things, some of them may not be valid but I love the institution of judiciary. I have spent more than 25 years of active life in the judiciary. It is because I love the institution that I find there are some infirmities, actually creeping into the institution. We must try to get rid of them so that the judiciary continues to project an image of being the dispenser of justice without fear or favour.

3

A JUDICIAL IMBROGLIO—A RESOLVENT SUBMISSION

V.R. Krishna Iyer

An issue has arisen affecting the highest judicial office of our country upon which it is difficult to speak, but impossible to remain silent. So I break my taciturnity briefly, reserving, for a later occasion, my creative, comprehensive critique of the judicial system, including justice, justices and justicing in their plural dimensions. The Judicature is too important an institution to be left solely to the Bench and the Bar. In the words of Laski:

> Obviously, therefore, the men who are to make justice in the courts, the way in which they are to perform their function, the methods by which they are to be chosen, the terms upon which they shall hold power, these, and their related problems, lie at the heart of political philosophy. When we know how a nation-state dispenses justice we know with some exactness the moral character to which it can pretend.

The people, as a whole, have a stake in the judicial process and, therefore, so vital an instrumentality as the Supreme Court must be regarded as a democratic institution with authority and accountability; and when 'something is rotten in the State of Denmark' and 'the time is out of joint', people have a right to know, to proffer proposals for reform and to ensure, through public discussion, panacean mutations in the system, subject, of course, to the critical needs of confidentiality, dignity and in camera hearing at strategic stages of investigation by high functionaries. A performance probe of the 'robed' syndrome—I include the Bench and the Bar—is no blasphemy but must be so seriously screened, scanned and operated as to comport with the eminence of judicial office and defence of its functional fundamentality. The proposition that judocracy is above interrogation and 'hands off' judges' obliquity and abuse of power are, in principle, incompatible with our Republic's values, although great care to forbid frivolity, malignity and misuse of opportunity and insistence on procedural fairness are imperative. 'In a democracy' says Judge Jerome Frank, in his classic 'Courts on Trial':

> It can ever be unwise to acquaint the public with the truth about the workings of any branch of government. It is wholly undemocratic to treat the public as children who are unable to accept the inescapable shortcomings of man-made institutions.... The best way to bring about the elimination of those shortcomings of our judicial system which are capable of being eliminated is to have all our citizens informed as to how that system now functions. It is a mistake, therefore, to try to establish and maintain, through ignorance, public esteem for our courts.

In sum, secrecy is allergy to democracy, including the judicial branch except in certain exceptional situations and in respect of some functionaries, although in a larger context and longer stretch of time, transparency is the rule and taciturnity the exception. There is no sound-proof system in an open society and, therefore, judicial affairs must also be an open book though *not open* to wilful scandalising or mala fide missiles.

The purpose at the present moment is very limited. Should delinquencies of judges be kept hidden for ever in the name of defending the integrity and credibility of the institution? An institution is what its members make it to be. If Parliamentarians are corrupt in large numbers there is no use saying that the criminality of such members should be banned from disclosure on the score that revelation of the truth is likely to bring Parliament into discredit. Nor can ministers claim immunity from their misdoings being investigatively brought to the notice of the public on the alibi that if the truth be known to the people they may lose faith in the Cabinet system. Likewise, if there are judicial culprits sullying the soul of the judicature why should the fact of the misbehaviour or venality be kept in the dark merely because when the people come to know that there are some blacksheep among the judicial flock, popular faith in the myth of majesty of the Court System is likely to be jeopardised. To wash institutions in the acid of truth is the way to remove the dross of lies. "Know ye the truth and the truth shall make you free." To suppress critical expression beyond minimal reticency parameters is to summon severe explosion of popular rage beyond the ineffectual power of contempt.

These general observations apart, what is urgent and pertinent at the moment is a single question straightforwardly to be met: whether *Satyameva Jayathe* is mere ritual chant or the bedrock of our Republic. In the past, some convulsive events affecting the Judiciary have taken place in Sri Lanka, Malaysia, Pakistan et al. India too has had corrupt instances and condign consequences *a la* Sinha J. (1964). Recently, some leading lawyers are reported to have presented a petition to the President of India setting out some 'charges' of misconduct against the seniormost puisne judge of the Supreme Court. If seniority were the monopoly criterion, he would be the successor to the present incumbent. The 'charges' are being gossiped about and discussed in the media on assumptions but no authentic source (the President, the Chief Justice or the alleged signatories have publicly released the accusations or their background and bases) has come to my notice. *The Statesman,* a responsible daily, has challengingly presented and critically scrutinised a string of allegations and the Supreme Court Bar Association has excitedly rejected them. In that sense, the accusations against this senior judge is public property. The accusing advocates persist in insisting that the judge is culpable and must forfeit his office while the defenders of the judge describe the charges as motivated, frivolous and fraught with damnatory impact on the holy institution. Newspaper reports or hearsay versions or bruits at Advocates' groups or claques may not be the foundation for great debate on so grave a matter as inculpates the seniormost Supreme Court Judge. Anyway, that is the way the country's functioning anarchy works. The story goes that the petition presented to the President has been made over to the Chief

Justice. These are confidential matters and, therefore, media reports and like sources cannot be taken to be conclusive testimony. But two meetings of the S.C. Bar Association and another meeting of the Bar Association of India appear to have polemised over the publicised charges. I had received a copy from Mr. P.P. Rao (for whom I have affectionate personal regard) of the gist of what he had spoken at the Bar Association meeting. I had also occasion to come across a brief report of the Bar Association of India's resolution wrongly reported by one daily as Mr. F.S. Nariman's statement, (so said Nariman, a distinguished lawyer, to me). The Chief Justice maintains a mystic and majestic silence and the judicial victim of the alleged venality keeps a sphinx-like muteness. For the people who have a right to know whether the imputations are grave or goofy, veracious or trumped up the current system offers no open sesame. For them, until some disinterested finding from an authoritative seat arrives or innovative alternative is adopted the whole episode is a 'riddle wrapped in a mystery inside an enigma.' Curiously enough, both the brethren sit on the same bench but why do the twain never meet and end the suspense? The Chief is the Chief and the next one, with long years' service in the Court, could easily discuss this delicate issue to the relief of the millions who look on the judicial camaraderie as a lovely reality and expect a resolution of this intra-mural imbroglio through a sensible *modus vivendi.*

When someone wants to charge a judge of the superior Courts with misbehaviour or incapacity, the Constitution provides for impeachment and lays down the process regulating this extraordinary measure. Our founding fathers had not foreseen and have not provided for anything less than impeachment for turpitudinous deviances. If the misbehaviour alleged is culpable but not grave enough to demand the dire step of impeachment what is the punitive process available? This virgin area of misconduct, short of misbehaviour or incapacity deserving of impeachment, remains a challenge for the creativity of Parliament. Supposing a string of charges were levelled against a judge and impeachment proceedings have not been initiated for some reason or other, a dilemmatic situation arises. A judicial culprit, in case there is evidence to substantiate the guilt, may not be left to Bar Association majorities or press indictments and their judgements one way or the other. While the Bar may well have a voice in assessment of a judge's worth, it may not be fair to entrust on Association of Advocates with the crucial power to pronounce a verdict about a judge. The remedy aggravates the malady. Inevitable lobbying and other toxic trends may pollute the atmosphere and affect the independence of judges. Even otherwise, many embarrassments will arise noxiously vitiating judicial dignity and forensic fairness. The level of bar debates, when the issue is emotive, is best left to lurid conjecture. Supposing the Bar Association pronounces one way or the other, scrambles for numbers and sound and fury in rivalry are not the adjudicatory highway to settle the fate of a judge. But then what is the alternative procedure to ventilate genuine grievances against a judge? Currently, there is none in India. Transfer of bad judges to other States is a placebo.

Our founding fathers have laid down for us a constitutional jurisprudence of judicial power, but in spite of their wisdom, the integral component of judicial accountability has not been designed with a sense of principled pragmatism. Of course, it is equally disconcerting that the legislators and the Executive have been indulging in corrupt and not-so-corrupt stultification of their vital functions. However, that is no alibi for judges to misbehave, especially because justice is the foremost human right and the first constitutional promise. Moreover, there is a spreading rash of judicial delinquency in many forms undreamt of in the past, unimaginable even today, and unprovided for by the founding fathers by way of correctional methodology. Luckily, the pathology is in the early stages and it is tragic that the disease is apparently showing up in the most unexpected quarters; and today from the highest court down to the floor level there is grievance writ large about forfeiture of confidence in judges for various reasons. The panache of wigs and robes, 'wise saws and modern instances', 'eyes severe and beard of formal cut', silver mace and liveried bearers cannot cover up the lost confidence and exposed culpability. Their lordships in full panoply will still invite attack unless they become institutionally and individually accountable to the country and be punishable for unbecoming behaviour, dereliction of duty and common criminality. Be you ever so high, the law, in its equal majesty, is above you too. The reasons for the decline are several but a most disturbing one of them is the absence of accountability and the frequency of unchecked abuse for anti-social and self-seeking purposes. Office and apparel are no amulets against detection and conviction. If we do not arrest the vice now, the institution may well be heading for collapse.

The judge is the symbol of justice itself and, therefore, we cannot have a dissection of private life and judicial life of the 'brethren'; both must become the sublime office. The pleasures and qualification of millionaires, the temptations and vices of the higher classes, the aberrations and abuses of persons in power are taboo or forbidden fruit for the judges. Winston Churchill, decades back, told the Commons that judges are required to conform to standards of "life and conduct far more severe and restricted than that of ordinary people."

The courts hold justly a highly, and unequalled pre-eminence in the respect of the world in criminal cases, and in civil cases; between man and man, no doubt, they deserve and command the respect and admiration of all classes of the community.

Indeed, their constitutional obligation to do justice without fear or favour, affection or ill will, is a high moral command and exacting demand on their conscience. If "you are what you wear" you have to keep up a certain manner of conduct which puts you in a category beyond the politicians and the members of the bureaucracy. Judges, like Caesar's wife, must be above suspicion. They must be patient, maintain poise, be gentle and impartial and decline to be provoked and never lapse into venal behaviour or class conscious uppishness. They must be truly free from communalism, regionalism, religionism and frequent acquaintance with alcohol and other deleterious contacts. These lapses are slowly creeping into the judicial 'brotherhood' even as factionalism and undignified wooing of ministers and party leaders are observably infecting justices and getting rewarded through appropriate 'elevations' and post-retiral 'life after death' offices. Unfortunately, the upstart breed and the midget species behave in violation of requisite rectitudes. On the bench they commit contempt by intemperate tongue; hubris, hauteur, highbrow airs and other sins of sadism which induce them to tease and insult and bring into ridiclue the judicial tenure itself. A code of conduct even on these details of decorum and comportment and dignified behaviour on the bench and in life may be necessary. Habitual violation must invite the displeasure of the law by punishment and reprimand. A bad judge with a wag's tongue or rude mood may do great harm to the institution.

In India some judges are stated to be notoriously communal, openly biased, foster favourites and have close relatives at the bar which factor leads to many improper practices. There are factions among judges which inflict mortal wounds on court justice. I agree with David Pannick in his observation:

> The student of the judiciary inevitably concludes that there have been many bad and some appalling judges, with all manner of defects, administering justice over the centuries.

I agree that "the place of justice is an hallowed place; and therefore, not only the bench, but the foot-pace and precincts thereof, out to be preserved without scandal and corruption" (Francis Bacon). Remember the opinion of David Pannick on this point:

> Litigants should have the power to refer to the (Judicial Performance) commission a complaint about the conduct of a judge. The Lord Chancellor should have such power, and should be obliged to exercise it prior to dismissing a judge. (This would not prevent a judge resigning to avoid publicity on the matter.) In May 1986, Lord Hailsham expressed support for the introduction of an independent complaints board to investigate the facts and make recommendations to the Lord Chancellor prior to the dismissal of a Circuit judge. He said (understandably) that he was troubled by the absence of a fair procedure at present.
>
> The jurisdiction of the commission would need to cover all members of the judiciary and should not be confined to cases where the Lord Chancellor is contemplating dismissal. Whoever the complainant may be, and however high the judicial status of the investigatee, the

value of the Commission would be in the presentation of a reasoned, public, and objective analysis of the relevant criteria and of the facts of the case.

A performance commission will impregnate the expression 'holding office during good behaviour' with living meaning.

Even judicial independence, a most important value of our system, cannot forbid bringing to book those guilty of judicial misbehaviour. Judge power is a critical factor of the highest importance in our constitutional order. For that very reason, the law must keep them away from lawless, immoral, unethical and unbecoming conduct. Some cowardly judges and opportunist brethren obligingly bend their judgements when political heavy-weights and tycoons with clout happen to be parties. Some leading members of the Supreme Court bar wrote, not long ago, a complaint to a Chief Justice referring to holiday hearings and nocturnal proceedings where influential persons figured as parties. Even the Bhopal Gas catastrophe litigation and later settlement with judicial imprimatur have come in for sharp criticism, bordering on the needle of suspicion being pointed at some judges. Why a hallowed Vigyan Bhavan becomes the venue for trial of a former Prime Minister?

In other countries, particularly in the U.S.A., there are specific statutes to deal with such situations which work well and do not victimise judges or dismiss light-heartedly serious aspersions. Confidentiality, trial by peers, *in camera* proceedings and other safeguards are built into the process in many countries. Thus, ensuring a remedy which will not inflict unjust indignity or reckless immunity may be availed of. Indian public law, vis-à-vis judicial culpability, is silent on this subject. It follows that Parliament must act by making suitable legislation, after due consultation with the Bench and the Bar, laying down the law regarding appointment, discipline and punitive handling of 'robed' misconduct. Perhaps, a Judicial Performance Commission, as advocated by David Pannick Q.C. (vide Judges), may be adopted with due adaptation to Indian conditions. But to get a wholesome enactment promptly legislated by Parliament is an exasperation under current confusing confrontations. Necessarily, therefore, misbehaviour and incapacity on the part of judges is a syndrome which can be controlled only by healthy conventions wrought carefully after serious discussion, reflection and wide consultations, reserving 'impeachment' more as constitutional terrorism 'red in tooth and claw' but in practice a politicised missile which stultifies the process and misses the purpose.

Some people would argue that judges should be bullet proof. I disagree. Because the Judiciary enjoys a security of tenure denied to politicians and unique among public servants. It is all the more necessary that judges should be subject to reasonable criticism of the performance of their duties. A person who has an arguable case that a judge has acted corruptly, maliciously or disgracefully cannot be told that the judge is protected by an iron curtain. Strong safeguards should be writ into the mechanism of enquiry so that judicial independence enjoys impervious defence against irresponsible attacks and irreversible publicity. Criticism is an occupational hazard where public functions of great moment are performed. Disappointed litigants shall never be able to shake the reputation or disturb the conscience of just judge. It must be remembered that unlike other public officers, the overwhelming majority of our judges do a difficult job extremely well but that does not destroy the case for a Judicial Performance Commission.

When any person levels a charge against a judge a solemn procedure must spring into operation. It must be presented, until a just legislation is enacted by Parliament forwarded to the President or the Chief Justice who, after being satisfied on his own—not by noises and numbers—that the matter needs to be scrutinised, may devise an in-house procedure serious, solemn and functionally worthy of the high office of judge and commanding consensus of the judiciary and otherwise strictly confidential lest the process be abused by blackmailing black-guards.

The present Chief Justice, a Judge with considerable experience at various levels and commanding respect from his peers, the bar and the public generally, may do well to consult his companion judges and such other judicial dignitaries as he deems fit and arrive at some broad consensus and adopt an in-house procedure composed of senior colleagues to deal with imputations *prima facie* amounting to misbehaviour. Of course, it must be made clear that newspaper publicity or public discussion of vicious charges against judges should be inhibited and the public told that there is an accessible, high-level and dignified remedial channel which may well be availed of by aggrieved or pro-bono individuals. Absent such a machinery, academic and media invigilation and indignant law criticism cannot be stifled, muted or intimidated. Just criticism is the oxygen of democracy. Silence is guilt where there is a duty to speak and judicial delinquency must suffer responsible exposure to the sunshine of sober publicity.

I gather that some such move is afoot and judicial statesmanship may well prevail in dealing with this delicate, difficult but necessary situation. Today, judicial imbroglio plagues the whole area and stinking instances proliferate in our society reeking with money market-friendly ethos. Blinking at it or burying one's head ostrich-like in the sands of supine indifference will not salvage the judiciary. Contempt Power is but impotent Maginot Line. Will it not be a proud day for the judges when they themselves claim with an awakened ethical response to the contemporary Moral Immuno-Deficiency Syndrome insidiously invading judicial probity that they are not above the law, that they *themselves* provide for control of integrity among the brethren and an in-house procedure is being devised to take suitable remedial action against judges who, by their acts and omissions, depart from the norms and values of judicial life. Indeed, independence of the Judiciary, according to U.N. accepted Basic Principles, implies that "Judges shall always conduct themselves in such a manner as to preserve the dignity of their office and the impartiality and independence of the Judiciary." Accountability goes with independence and misbehaviour breaches public trust and accountability. Art. 8 of the Basic Principles on the Independence of Judiciary expressly states this *desideratum*. Art. 17 reads thus: A charge or complaint made against a Judge in his/her judicial and professional capacity shall be processed expeditiously and fairly under an appropriate procedure. The judge shall have the right to a fair hearing. The examination of the matter at its initial stage shall be kept confidential, unless otherwise requested by the Judge. Judges, when charged, are entitled to justice according to the high standards of their office. The finer thought which Winston Churchill in lovely diction, told the House of Commons "that judges are required to conform to standards of life and conduct far more severe and restricted than that of ordinary people." "What', the Prime Minister asked rhetorically, "would be thought of a Lord Chief Justice if he won the Derby?"

The current controversy about a senior judge is not my business. The Bar can be victim of lobbying and counter-campaigning but that is their business. Moreover, impeachment relates to misconduct or incapacity and removal of the judge, whether he be an associate Judge or a Chief Justice. The immediate problem is different, viz. whether the seniormost judge is not worthy of being elevated to the highest judicial office. If, in the meanwhile, someone, satisfying the Constitutional calculus for impeachment, moves the Speaker/Chairman the situation has its own political dialectic and dynamic fall-out. No view needs expression on the justice of such a strategy and justification of the grounds in the given context. Impeachment is meant to meet rarer delinquencies. The leaders of such a move are people of sagacity but should not falter lest it should backlash. Let us cerebrate with a little specificity.

To fill that exalted office is to entrust him with the functions of the highest office in the country in terms of judicial power which is the vastest in the world. The Chief Justice of India is a sublime symbol of a noble office, a seat of commanding height and not merely the seniormost member of the judicial fraternity. The halo, supremacy and power must be matched by the eminence par excellence of the 'ermined' personality of the Chief Justice. This is a tall demand not answered merely by calendrical seniority. More is needed than length of service. But, in the absence of a profoundly impartial assessment by a nationally accepted judicial commission, we have to go by pedestrians standards such as length of service and absence of *pronounced unworthiness.* Arbitrariness in choice violates the Constitution's voice.

The superior status and commanding height of the office of the Chief Justice of India, even though his judicial powers are no higher than those of his colleagues, makes it a matter of great moment to assess, with responsible sensitivity and delicate care, the fitness of the successor to the office when the present incumbent retires. Supersession of the seniormost has historically acquired the odium of Executive authoritarianism. The convention has grown that the sitting Chief Justice makes a recommendation regarding his successor and this is reflected in the judgement of the 9 Judges, especially of Verma, J. It behoves the sitting C.J. to exercise his power of recommendation, an unwritten convention, with a high sense of detached judgement. His judicial conscience in evaluating his successor's qualities, not as a judge, which he already is, but as a superleader cannot be casual or mechanical but must be the product of mature reflection undeflected by subjective impressionism, extraneous factors or the voice of a clique. Other things being equal, in the absence of anything to brand the seniormost puisne judge as unfit to be the commander of the judicial legion (not in ordering about or bullying which he cannot, but in his moral authority and high bearing) he may be recommended. A pedestrian to be a stop-gap C.J. for a narrow spell of a week or two is not a commendable convention. However, if there is something substantive affecting his worth, moral stature and impeccably lofty character, enmeshed in serious controversy, he should not ordinarily be the natural successor. This is a delicate area when the benefit of doubt must go in favour of the seniormost. But in a case where charges have been raised and unfortunately bandied about at the Bar, in the Press and among the public, embroiling the name in acrimonious controversy, one expects the retiring Chief Justice to bestow conscientious scrupulosity in assessing the worth of his successor, not from the point of his judicial ability which, one must assume, he does possess but from the different and higher angle of sitting at the Everest of the Indian Judicature. Fitness is a blend of functional eminence, untainted character, a presence that impresses and a personality that repels suppliance or pressure from inside or outside, however high the source or powerful the threat or temptation. The Chief must not mix himself with impeachment issues which are largely left to the Hon'ble Speaker/Chairman of either House, properly approached. Other considerations like political links, shameful but concealed blemishes or suspicious foreign nexus are matters for consideration by the Prime Minister. The President will make his decision with respectful consideration of the C.J.I's views, and the P.M's suggestions if any. A certain transparency and wider consultation strengthen the wisdom of the final choice.

Finally and most importantly, I think the Judges of the Supreme Court or at least the Chief Justice conference must consider these issues of profound national importance among themselves frankly and informally. The C.J. must be recognised as the Chief and, in administrative matters, the leader. The Judge against whom imputations are made is a senior brother Judge and, in the true spirit of brotherhood, it would be fair to expect him to meet his own Chief and clarify his point of view, explain the allegations against him and clear the ground for the Chief justice to form his opinion with the added satisfaction that he has had a fraternal, friendly meeting of minds whatever the outcome. It is just and proper for the Chief to give a full and deferential hearing to his seniormost brother *if he seeks a hearing, as he should.* If brotherhood among the judges has meaning, the proper thing to do, in a disciplined body, is for the judge against whom charges have been levelled to call on the Chief and have the matter freely, frankly and fully discussed. There is no element of *infra dig* here but an affirmation of fraternity, mutual respect and recognition of the Chief as the Chief and the other as brother. The Chief must naturally give due weight to his brother's explanations; and unless the gravamen of the charges is too serious, the camaraderie of the S.C. Judiciary must be preserved as a finer bond of felicitious fellowship.

To conclude by expressing the view that No. 2 must meet No. 1 in a spirit of cordiality and No. 1 must greet such an opportunity for closed door discussion and resolution of what might otherwise end up as an institutional explosion. A senior judge, close to the Chief Justice, would not wish to tarnish his image at the critical hour of his proximity to the highest judicial post. In his own interest and of the nation all blemishes should be washed white. To shrink from this minimal measure throws suspicion on the appointee. To be cleared by his peers makes him deserve the acme of the curial pyramid. Any dubious aloofness, punctilious prestigiousness or supercilious charade prompting the ego of a brother judge in not calling on the Chief Justice is an indiscretion subverting the institutional leadership of the Summit Court, whoever be the Chief protem. Court camaraderie is the paradigm, its factionalism is sabotage of its integrity and groupism is the beginning of the end. The Chief is the first among equals and the Constitution recognises it.

Before long, a National Judicial Commission, beyond the incestuous composition of and interaction among judges themselves, is the *desideratum.* Statesmanship summons high level participation in such a Performance Commission. The way in which 'Judge and Co.' (Jeremy Bentham's phrase for the Judiciary) is run is a matter of public interest and national scrutiny.

The long-term agenda of Judicial Reform and Forensic Five Year Plans for activising the instrumentality must be relegated to a different occasion but is important and urgent. To tarry or tinker is to commit hara-kiri, dear brethren. The noblest office must be filled by the finest judge, seniority being a great, though not the only determinant.

That is the dharma of that lofty office and, may be, if the alleged imputations against No. 2 are screened confidentially and cleared after the seniormost brother has met and clarified, the cloud is, likely to be banished and the installation follows. Impeachment is another street, the operators are different and the *modus operandi* has a political flavour. Personalities do not count when our 'justice patriotism' holds high the banner on which is inscribed the thought Tennyson has poetized:

"A land of settled government,
A land of just and old renown,
Where Freedom slowly broadens down
From precedent to precedent."

4

SOME REFLECTIONS ON THE PROBLEMS OF THE INDIAN JUDICIARY

V.R. Krishna Iyer

Social Justice is the signature tune of our Constitution and as Capelletti has insisted in his classic work 'access to Justice is the foremost human right'. The mensuration of the Indian Justice system as a triumph or tragedy is by using the yardstick of meaningful delivery of justice, equity and good conscience to every member of Indian humanity. That is the quintessence of our Founding Deed.

Our court system is at once glorious and inglorious and needs, from a dialectical angle, serious changes if it is to slough off the imperial weaknesses of Raj vintage and assimilate the democratic imperatives of Republic mintage. A new synthesis, in harmony with the vibrant conscience of the Constitution and the values of the New World Human Order, is the urgent *desideratum.* A social audit of the performance of our system, including its top echelons and floor-level cadres, is a necessary democratic exercise. Judges are not the voice of infallibility and must, like other institutions of our Republic, submit to public scrutiny by jurists, invigilation by socially sensitive peers and be broadly accountable to the collective sovereign, the people of India. David Pannic in his book *Judges* has explained in felicitious prose the flawless logic of judges being judged:

> Some politicians, and a few jurists, urge that it is unwise or even dangerous to tell the truth about the judiciary. Judge Jerome Frank of the US Court of Appeals sensibly explained that he had little patience with, or respect for, that suggestion. I am unable to conceive.... that, in a

> democracy, it can never be unwise to acquaint the public with the truth about the workings of any branch of government. It is wholly undemocratic to treat the public as children who are unable to accept the inescapable shortcomings of man-made institutions.... The best way to bring about the elimination of those shortcomings of our judicial system which are capable of being eliminated is to have all our citizens informed as to how that system now functions. It is a mistake, therefore, to try to establish and maintain, through ignorance, public esteem for our courts.

Surely the way in which 'Judge & Co.' administer judicial business is a matter of people's concern and therefore of public debate. The rule of law is a basic feature of our Constitutional Order but remember, the rule of law is not the rule of lawyers even as the supremacy of the Constitution is not the supremacy of Judges. Lawyers judge Judges and the country holds the Bench and Bar to social scrutiny. When I retired from the Supreme Court, some distinguished Advocates affectionately gave me a fairwell address where, in decorative diction, they stated:

> Permit us to remind you that the bar is the judge of judges and no judge can avoid or escape the verdict of the bar. We have summoned you this evening to hear our unanimous declaratory verdict. Our verdict is a decree of affection and admiration. Let us also declare, in these proceedings which are suit generis, that we are not only your judges but also your judgement-debators.

Often in pensive mood or intervals of introspection, I reflect on the quality of judges and lawyers and feel unhappy when I hear 'the still, sad music of humanity', victimised by injustice with nothing to console them except the round ocean and the blue sky. We want good Judges and good lawyers if a fine justice system is to be the solace of the multitude of actual and potential litigants. A poem by Elizabeth, Wordsworth has a realism about the operators of the legal system:

"If all the good people were clever,
And all clever people were good,
The world would be nicer than ever
We thought that it possibly could.
But somehow, 'tis seldom or never
The two hit it off as they should;
The good are so harsh to the clever,
The clever so rude to the good!"

The Bar watchdogs the judges and renders verdicts at times. These days many bizarre changes are wrought. The members of the profession turn militant and mobilise for collective action against judicial dereliction and delinquency and even resort to aggressive agitation and beyond. At times thoroughly selfish interests drive some lawyers to block measures essential for public justice and common weal. The nation, under hitherto unknown shocks, has woken up to the horrendous issues of back-breaking backlog and logjam of dockets, the most disgraceful in history, unbecomingly brash, unbearably arrogant behavioural degeneracy of the judiciary, the callousness and neglect, the medievalism and obsolescent technology, the managerial backwardness and authoritarian attributes of the judicial process, product and personnel. Above all, the very modus of appointments to the high judicial offices, the political pollution in the selection method, the secrecy and sinister influences and absence of any public screening or moral scanning procedures—these have come up for public scrutiny. The old values which made judges the nation's proud asset suddenly got demonetised, corrupt currency became common. Judges began to form factions, became regional and communal, promoted personal advancement by lobbying, turned professionally avaricious, and justice *by* judges, *for* judges through judicial process, even judicial interest litigation, made their unblushing appearance.

The present generation of lawyers and judges, with a considerable number of splendid exceptions, is moving downhill towards professionally amoral, even immoral mores; shocking revelations about judges, rare to begin with but recurring with unhappy frequency, make the pernicious praxis first a whisper, then a wild rumour and then, by deepening degrees, a proven deed, an investigated act, a vice in the womb of the robed fraternity! *Many, most members are pure even now.* The few are no longer few and are enough in numbers and deeds to debunk the credibility and liquidate the sublimity of the judiciary. The other joint tort-feasor, the dubious lawyer, who is the corrupter, the traitor, the enemy of the Bar, is surfacing in a swelling stream.

Thank God, only a miniscule fraction is infected by this contageous disease. But the immune system will fail altogether as an AID syndrome if the whole professional morality, probity and efficiency is not utterly overhauled and at once.

The lawyer of yesterday is the judge of today and is raised to the higher courts tomorrow. The guilt by association is easy to transmit from the bar to the bench and this ongoing process is at work. Before every judicial deviant is a lawyer delinquent. Judges had disciplinary powers over lawyers, but for good or ill, autonomy is now the rule. But the aberrations of professional autonomy are so many that a campaign for cardiac surgery of the wicked is now on. If the bar fails, the bench will break and the morale of the people will pale. Likewise, the independence of the lawyer, who fights a cause, is a treasured value. The finest calibre of the bar is a *sine qua non* of the glory of justice. No judiciary can reach its peaks of performance without the bedrock of a public-spirited bar with priceless value commitments and human compassion.

If judges and lawyers decay the cause of justice collapses. *Coprruptio optimi pessima* (The corruption of the best is the worst of all).

The background to the administration of social justice in our Socialist Republic is important since the Court has already held that the rule of law, socialism and secularism are inviolable, unamendable, and integral to the basic structure of the Constitution. A relevant observation by Chinnappa Reddy J. speaking for the Court in *AIR 1982 SC 879* runs thus:

> Now, thanks to the rising social and political consciousness and the expectations roused as a

consequence and the forward looking posture of this Court, the underprivileged also are clamouring for their rights and are seeking the intervention of the Court with touching faith and confidence in the Court. The Judges of the Court have a duty to redeem their constitutional oath and do justice no less to the pavement dweller than to the quest of the Five Star Hotel.

Justice Desai strengthened the socialist content of the Constitution by a few clear observations:

> Recall at this stage the preamble, the floodlight illuminating the path to be pursued by the State to set up a Sovereign Socialist Secular Democratic Republic. Expression 'socialist' was intentionally introduced in the Preamble by the Constitution (Forty-Second Amendment) Act, 1976. In the objects and reasons for amendment amongst other things, ushering in of socio-economic revolution was promised. The clarion call may be extracted:
>
> The question of amending the Constitution for removing the difficulties which have arisen in achieving the objective of socio-economic revolution, which would end poverty and ignorance and disease and inequality of opportunity, has been engaging the active attention of Government and the public for some time....
>
> It is, therefore, proposed to amend the Constitution to spell out expressly the high ideals of socialism.... to make the directive principles more comprehensive....

What does a Socialist Republic imply? Socialism is a much misunderstood word. Values determine contemporary socialism, pure and simple. But it is not necessary at this stage to go into all its ramifications. The principal aim of a socialist State is to eliminate inequality in income and status and standards of life. The basic framework of socialism is to provide a decent standard of life to the working people and especially provide security from cradle to grave. This amongst others on economic side envisaged economic equality and equitable distribution of income. This is a blend of Marxism and Gandhism leaning heavily towards Gandhian socialism.

If language has meaning, the semantic thrust of Parts III, IV and IV A of the Constitution is obvious. A radical conceptualisation of social justice is luminously presented here. Judges, as also the operators of the other two instrumentalities of the State, must remember Social, Economic and Political Justice to every Indian is the first promise of the Sovereign Republic, and it is the plainest duty, the fundamental oath of office of judges not to betray the Constitution which is the only instrument from where they weave and wear the robe of authority. In this context, Art. 32 is a unique provision rare to find in any other Constitution, calls for emphasis because the infantile alibi of arrears of cases has been used by honest Justices, anaemically deficient in the passion of the Constitution to defend people's fundamental rights as the supreme sentinel on the *qui vive,* to cut down Art. 32 to conform to judicial convenience and to violate a paramount mandate and let down the little Indian who seeks justice direct from the Supreme Court because that remedy is *guaranteed.* The citizen has the right to this guaranteed remedy; the court has a power to grant that remedy and that high power carries a correspondingly solemn duty. No sophistry can extricate the Court from this functional compulsion. Indeed, in rulings of the Supreme Court. Art. 32 has been held to be an important and integral part of the basic structure of the Constitution and the judges, without breach of oath and forfeiture of office, cannot play hide and seek with this guaranteed right.

Dr. Ambedkar, in emphatic diction, stressed the critical importance of Art. 32:

> Now, Sir, I am very glad that the majority of those who spoke on this article have realised the importance and the significance of this article. If I was asked to name any particular Article in this Constitution as the most important—an Article without which this Constitution would be a nullity—I could not refer to any other Article except this one. It is the very soul of the Constitution

and the very heart of it and I am glad that the House has realised its importance.

(In the Constituent Assembly on 9-12-48)

This unique right of the citizen to secure judicial enforcement and the Court's high power to direct enforcement of Part III Rights, are themselves 'Constitutional remedies', placed in the paramount category of Fundamental Rights. And paramountcy is paramountcy, which cannot be dethroned to the status of discretionary remedies, whatever the pressure on judicial time or rationale of forcing parties to move the High Court first before invoking Art. 32—an option which will give judges a procrastination but land the urgent litigant in loss of time and money. In Court versus Constitution, sound jurisprudence obviously directs the judges not to seek superiority.

But though the Constitution is what the judges say it is, the court itself is *under* the Constitution, not *over* it and must advance, not abase its purpose and promise. A solitary aberration, however appealing to overworked judges, cannot dilute the mandatory temper of Art. 32. It is a different matter if no fundamental right is directly involved in the case.

It is true that the Supreme Court has diluted Art. 32 by injecting a discretionary element into the mandatory provision. The burden of the Judges dockets, *if Art. 32 is a categorical imperative,* is no alibi for ingenious circumvention. True, the Supreme Court is final, but not infallible and someday a more conscientious Bench will restore Art. 32 and Citizen's Fundamental Rights beyond Judicial manoeuvres. To despatch a party aggrieved, who invokes Art. 32 making out a case of breach of his fundamental right, to the High Court and later again to the Supreme Court is multiplication of litigation, delaying justice by doubling the process and obviously making access to the Supreme Court, avoidably expensive—a dubious judicial dexterity and a remedy that aggravates the malady. "Ye are the salt of the earth: but if the salt have lost its savour wherewith shall it be salted?" The Court must be moved to reconsider this truncation of Art. 32, and Parliament must pass a unanimous resolution expressing concern about this fundamental right being rendered a discretionary pleasure of the judges.

Like Justice Thakkar, Justice Venkataramaiah strongly advocated parties going to the High Courts, as against the Supreme Court, to reduce the crowd of dockets in the Supreme Court so as to dispose of "old matters in which parties are crying for relief."

In this context, the High Courts are praised by the Supreme Court Judges only to justify jettisoning Art. 32 petitions from the Supreme Court. If the High Courts are so rich in talents why have a Supreme Court? Why all the scramble to be elevated to the summit Court? To me this flattery of High Court Justices is a 'tongue-in-cheek' argument. Our High Courts are weighed down to sinking level with arrears and there too, litigants are crying for justice. In short, to rewrite the Constitution by dethrowning Art. 32 is to show scant respect to the Constituent Assembly. The straightforward way is to devise radical methods of tackling docket explosion which distressingly accumulates and virtually asphyxiates dispensing of justice *at every level.*

What do we say about judges who delay pronouncement of judgements for months and years? Judges of the High Courts are more culpable in this respect, being immune to action by any higher authority and protected from criticism because of distorted ideas about contempt of Court jurisprudence. One activist judge with an efficient assistant, as in America, and technological instruments at his service can turn out what five Judges now do in any Court. Computers for the Bench and the Bar with versatile skills, reduce oral arguments and quite a number of other changes, including training for Judges in Court Management, will go a long way in controlling the mounting arrears in Courts. Where is there a national discussion or seminar with *judges, lawyers, technologists and management specialists sitting together* to design concrete steps to deal with this himalayan problem? A grocer's shop has more technology than a magistrate's court. Not even a regularly working photocopier is available in the Courts with the result an elementary system of getting copies quickly even of judgements and decrees is functional in our near—21st century and MNCs invading our country with fast foods.

The common argument of the Court being flooded with Art. 32 petitions cannot be used to weaken citizen's fundamental rights. Remedies have to be sought elsewhere, not by interdict on a fundamental right. Indeed, the same floodgate argument has been conveniently adopted to shut out public interest litigations. To my mind, this captions ground is indirectly a criticism of the Constitution and its makers. When people are conscious, as they should be, of their basic rights they should be encouraged to seek redress in court rather than in the street. The same Supreme Court has extended or rather created a strange jurisdiction by a strained interpretation of Art. 142. The founding fathers knew of the difference between the High Court and the Supreme Court while enacting Arts. 32 and 226. Docket-phobic allergy cannot ban and bolt the Courts' doors when poor litigants come to the highest Court under a specific jurisdiction based on a special jurisprudence. And, after all, even by denying access under Art. 32 what is the disposal rate of the Supreme Court during the last decade, with escalating arrears, exasperating delays in hearing and shocking distance between closing of the hearing and delivery of the judgement? The system has broken down, according to some Chief Justice who have addressed the Supreme Court Bar Association on Law Day. Of course, in recent years, the Chief Justices have been conscientising the Court's functions and technologising its processes. Many things can be done for dispensation of justice with inexpensive and early finality. I will make a few suggestions later, but here, with due respect to the great Judges, I dissent from the negative attitude towards Art. 32—(Vide AIR 1987 SC 1159—Kanubhai Brahmbhatt's Case).

To jettison Justice, in its social dimensions, because the judge is apprehensive of overloading of legal cargo or logjam of dockets is, to 'talaq' yourself from the office which gives you power. The critical importance of judicial perceptions and perspectives of social justice is so challenging that this creative judicial functionalism needs to be stressed as integral to the constitutional process. Indeed, a radical judiciary is the locomotive of the constitutional revolution our founding fathers envisioned.

The hues of history, the urges of the swaraj struggle, the blood and tears of the primitive masses and the silent suffering of the tortured gender and bonded labour help concretise what is social injustice to obliterate which was the objective of Independence.

Said Nehru long years ago:

> The service of India means the service of the millions who suffer. It means the ending of poverty and ignorance and disease and inequality of opportunity. The ambition of the greatest man of our generation has been to wipe every tear from every eye. That may be beyond us, but as long as there are tears and suffering, so long our work will not be over.

Dr. Ambedkar addressing the Constituent Assembly finally emphasises:

> On the social plane, we have in India a society based on the principle of graded inequality which means elevation of some and degradation for others. On the economic plane, we have a society in which there are some who have immense wealth as against many who live in abject poverty. On the 26th January 1950, we are going to enter into a life of contradictions.
>
> In our social and economic life we shall, by reason of our social and economic structure, continue to deny the principle of one man one value. How long shall we continue to live this life of contradictions? How long shall we continue to deny equality in our social and economic life? If we continue to deny it for long, we will do only by putting our political democracy in peril. We must remove this contradiction at the earliest possible moment or else those who suffer from inequality will blow up the structure of political democracy which this Assembly has so laboriously built up.

My meaning is deepened if I recall a dialogue between Gurudev Tagore and Mahatma Gandhi since it is instructive for judges charged by a compassionate constitution to hasten the peaceful process of transformation of the Indian Human Order to accord with the values enwombed in the noble Preamble which is a basic feature of the Constitution. Now to the Gurudev Bapuji exchange:

> Once Gurudev Rabindranath Tagore asked Gandhiji:
>
> "Gandhiji are you so unromantic? When in the early dawn, the morning sun rises, does it not fill your heart with joy to see its reddish glow? When the birds sing does not your heart thrill with its divine music? When the rose opens its petals and blooms in the garden does its sights not bring cheer to your heart?
>
> The Mahatma replied, "Gurudev, I am not so dumb or insensitive, as not to be moved by the beauty of the rose or the morning rays of the sun or the divine music of the birds. But what can I do? My one desire, my one anxiety, my one ambition is when shall I see the red tint of the rose on the cheeks of hungry naked millions of my people? When shall I hear the sweet and melodious song of the birds in place of their agonising sighs? When will such music come out of their soul and when will that day come when the light of the morning sun will illumine the heart of the common man in India? When will I see its lustre and brightness on his face?"

Constitutional jurisprudence is woven from life's realities articulated by great thinkers, no opportunist politicians. The warp and woof of our Constitution is the life, liberty and pursuit of happiness by the suffering members of Indian humanity.

The quintessence of justice, in the contemplation of the Constitution, is the liberation from socio-economic subjection and consists in the actualisation of the goal of "full and free development of every individual", to use the words of Karl Marx in *Das Capital*. For the Indian Constitution the holistic conception of freedom is of supreme relevance. Indeed, the International Human Rights Conference in Teheran (1968), called by the General Assembly of the United Nations, one of the most significant of its kind to date, declared in a final proclamation:

> Since human rights and fundamental freedoms are indivisible, the full realisation of civil and political rights without the enjoyment of economic, social and cultural rights, is impossible.

This integrality has been stressed again and again.

In the same strain Justice Gajendragadkar in *Workers of Gold Mines case (AIR 1958 S.C. 923)* summed up the response of an aware court:

> Social and economic justice have been given a place of pride in our Constitution and one of the directive principles of State policy enshrined in Article 38 requires that the State shall strive to promote the welfare of the people by securing and protecting as effectively as it may a social order in which justice—social, economic and political—shall inform all the institutions of national life. The concept of social and economic justice is a living concept of revolutionary import, it gives sustenance to the rule of law and meaning and significance to the ideal of a Welfare State.

The judges have a role in transforming people's frustrations into a revolution of expectations of a humane tomorrow.

The dialectic of the rule of law arises from the obvious contradiction of two forces:

The first, the colonial factor, drags the country back; the second, the swaraj urge, spells the need for a revolution forward. From the juxtaposition of these two paradoxical presences follows the third compulsion that if Justice is an inalienable right of the millions of Indian people, with their chronic social squalor, ubiquitous poverty and massive illiteracy, its meaningful fulfilment is a pledge to our future and necessitates many radical changes in the system of law and justice, viewed as a larger undertaking. Lord Denning, looking at the Indian Court, has said in passing:

> Law does not stand still. It moves continually. Once this is recognised, then the task of the Judge is put on a higher plane. He must consciously seek to mould the law so as to serve the needs of the time. He must not be a mere mechanic, a mere working mason, laying brick

> on brick, without thought to the overall design. He must be an architect—thinking of the structure as a whole—building for society a system of law which is strong, durable and just. It is on his work that civilised society itself depends.

Wigs and gowns and the cult of the robes are no substitute for a revolutionary theory of constitutional justice. Granville Austin, in his great work on the Constitution of India, asserts that the judiciary was considered by the founding fathers to be an instrument for engineering the constitutional revolution; but, having regard to the court pyramid's actual performance a pessimistic verdict that the judges have partially failed, is difficult to avoid.

The butcher, the baker, the candlestick maker, the bonded labourer, the pavement dweller, the damsel in distress, the sweated worker, the starving child, the dalit, the tribal and the socio-economic pariah shall have a vested interest in the Republic, only if the Constitution has a vested interest in their survival, their human worth and personhood.

The unconscious assumptions, the inarticulate politics and the *status quo* thinking, learnt as young law students and hardened in the elite school of life, are not easy to overcome. Judges must, therefore, consent to a course on *Justice under the Constitution,* washing away many interpretive distortions imported by precedents laid down by the pride of great judicial lions who, at best, were liberal, and, at worst, idolators of dated dogmas, and hardly ever, iconoclasts with radical thought.

Jawaharlal Nehru, while inaugurating the Conference organised by the International Commission of Jurists (I.C.J) in Delhi, urged that the rule of law must run close to the rule of life. The I.C.J. in its declaration of Delhi, at that conference incorporated the same idea:

> The Rule of Law is a dynamic concept for the expansion and fulfilment of which jurists are primarily responsible and which should be employed not only to safeguard and advance the civil and political rights of the individual in a free society, but also to establish social, economic,

educational and cultural conditions under which his legitimate aspirations and dignity may be realized.

(I.C.J. Declaration of Delhi)

Decisions of Courts often reflect the judges, philosophy, conditioned by the values of the Constitution which is the paramount factor more important than the particular views of Judges pro tem. Even so, Constitutional jurisprudence has to be realistic and cannot be an omnipotence in the sky. Judges must therefore take into consideration the basic structure and features of the Constitution, as interpreted by the Judges. For instance, the Preamble to our Constitution which describes India as a Sovereign Secular Socialist Democratic Republic is a basic feature which is inviolable. So much so, the Court, as the sentinel of the power process, must control and guide the development of policies consonant with the parameters laid down in the Preamble.

5

ROLE OF JUDGES

Prem Kumar

The task of the judge is to give meaning to constitutional values and he does that by working with the constitutional text, history and social ideals.... The function of a judge is to give concrete meaning and application to our constitutional values. The task of a judge...... should be seen as giving meaning to our public values and adjudication as the process through which that meaning is revealed or elaborated...... I doubt whether dispute resolution is an adequate description of the social function of courts. To my mind, courts exist to give meaning to our public values, not to resolve disputes. Constitution adjudication is the most vivid manifestation of the function.

OWEN FISS

Judicial Alertness

In recent years the Indian Judiciary has shown itself up as the only really functioning arm of the Constitution. The judges have helped magnify the majesty of law and have been instrumental in the process of the law adapting itself commensurate to the needs of the changing times. Many landmark decisions on matters of public interest, like those relating to environmental issues, greater transparency and accountability of administration, have made an enduring impact on the society. From corruption to crime, corporate disputes to human rights and activating the law enforcing agencies to disciplining the general public, the courts have played a pivotal role in all fields for achieving the goal of social cleansing. The courts are now seen as the last resort for the oppressed and the bewildered. During the golden jubilee year of the Indian Constitution, the basic tenet of Rule of Law: Be you ever so high, the law is above you was kept high. The ever vigilant courts have been spreading new light on the Constitution providing great constitutional protection to the public from the unlimited range of vagaries of the bureaucratic culture.

The courts have been more attentive to correcting executive actions of the sort for their unreasonableness, particularly in administrative matters.

The law has been used as an instrument of justice. The court is augmenting its support base and moral authority at a time when other institutions of government are facing a legitimation crisis.

The PIL

The PIL (Public Interest Litigation) action by various groups has brought a general awakening amongst various depressed, oppressed and suppressed sections of the society, giving a ray of hope in the improvement of their lot through the court process. Enough has already been done in the field of human rights, and in particular to the right to life. From undertrials and convicted prisoners to bonded and migrant labourers to dalits, unorganised agricultural labourers, landless and untouchables slum-dwellers and victims of all types including vulnerable groups like juvenile and women have got awakened and approach the courts as judicial power is being used increasingly to ameliorate the miseries of masses.

The procedural laws enacted by the legislature and the rules of practise evolved by the judiciary regulate the procedure in the courts. The preliminary question that the courts consider is that of locus standi, i.e., the legal capacity to institute the proceedings. From the traditional approach where the courts concede locus standi only to aggrieved person or a member or a group of persons from the public having 'sufficient interest' in the subject matter, the courts have shown a readiness to abandon the concept of honfeldian plaintiff in favour of the ideological plaintiff.

In *Fertilizer Corpn. Kamgar Union vs. UOI AIR 1981 SC 344* the apex court through Justice Iyer observed:

Law, as I conceived it is a social auditor and this audit function can be put into action only when someone with real public interest ignites the jurisdiction. We cannot be scared by the fear that all and sundry will be litigation-happy and waste their time and money and the time of the court through false and frivolous cases. In a society where freedoms suffer from atrophy and activism is essential for participative public justice, some risks have to be taken and more opportunities opened for the public-minded citizen to rely on the legal process and not be repelled from it by narrow pedantry now surrounding locus standi.

In Transfer of Judges cases *(S.P. Gupta vs. President of India AIR 1982 SC 149)* the seven-judge Bench adopted the liberal approach. Justice P.N. Bhagwati observed:

What is sufficient interest to give standing to a member of the public would have to be determined by the Court in each individual case. It is not possible for the Court to lay down any hard and fast rule or any strait-jacket formula for the purpose of defining or delimiting 'sufficient interest'. It has necessarily to be left to the discretion of the court. The reason is that in a modern complex society which is seeking to bring about transformation of its social and economic structure and trying to reach social justice to the vulnerable sections of the people by creating new social, collective 'diffuse' rights and interests and imposing new public duties on the state and other public authorities, infinite number of situations are bound to arise which cannot be imprisoned in a rigid mould or a procrustean formula. The Judge who has the correct social perspective and who is on the same wavelength as the Constitution will be able to decide, without any difficulty and in consonance with the constitutional objectives, whether a member of the public moving the court in a particular case has sufficient interest to initiate the action.

In 1982, the Supreme Court received letter along with a clipping of the newspaper 'Indian Express' dated Aug. 26, 1982 bringing to the notice of the Court that a large number of migrant workmen were subjected to exploitation and violation of various welfare laws made for them. The Court intervened by treating the letter as a writ petition under Art. 32. Directions were issued to the Labour Commissioner (Centre) to enquire into and submit a report; the Central Government was also asked to file their affidavit. In this case reported in *Salal Hydro Project vs. State of J&K & others (1983) 2 SCC 181* the Court found that the workmen were denied of the minimum wages and other welfare benefits. Accordingly directions were given.

Dr. Upendra Baxi noted Jurist and Humanist addressed a letter to the Supreme Court requesting for protecting the girls living in the Government Protective Homes at Agra who were being denied right to live with basic human dignity by the State of U.P. running the Home. The Apex Court in the case of *Dr. Upendra Baxi and others vs. State of U.P. and others (1986) 4 SCC 106* held that the public interest litigation involves a collaboration and cooperative efforts by the State Government and its officers, the lawyers appearing in the case and the Bench for the purpose of making Human Rights meaningful for the weaker sections of the community in ensuring the socio-economic justice to the deprived and the vulnerable sections of the humanity in the country.

In *Vincent Panikuriangera vs. Union of India & others (1987) 2 SCC 1651* the Court pointed out that the statutory bodies and the government are bound to respond and join the proceedings pending before the Court. They do not have the choice of keeping away from the Court like private parties in ordinary litigation opting to go ex-parte. The Court held that Public Interest Litigation is not a normal litigation with adversaries pitted against one another. As the matter involved health of the public, the court ensured cooperation of all the parties and suo moto extended the opportunity of hearing and inviting the named statutory authorities to assist the Court.

In *Rural Litigation and Entitlement Kandra vs. State of U.P. (1989) supp. 1. SCC 504* the Court dealt with a PIL relating to ecological imbalances created due to mining operations and denudation of forest. The Court directed the stoppage of mining activity as it created ecological imbalance and denudation of the forest.

In *M.C. Mehta & another vs. UOI & others (1989) 1. SCC 395* the Constitution Bench considered the scope of PIL to grant compensation to the victims of hazardous or dangerous activities when death or injuries were caused to them on account of the accident during the operation of such activities. The Court held that the law should keep pace with changing socio-economic norms. Where a law of the past does not fit in the present context, the court should evolve a new law in a public interest litigation. The Court held that its power was very wide to devise appropriate procedure and to issue directions, orders or rules. The Court is competent to grant a remedial assistance by way of compensation in exceptional cases. The Court has incidental and ancillary power in exercise of which it can devise new methods and strategy in securing enforcement of fundamental rights particularly in public interest litigation or social action cases. Directions accordingly issued.

In *Bandhua Mukti Morcha vs. UOI & others (1984) 3 SCC 161* the letter addressed to the court was treated as a writ petition. The court took the assistance of the parties, got the evidence collected and then issued appropriate directions for release of the bonded labour. The court held that when the poor come before the court particularly for enforcement of their fundamental rights, it is necessary to depart from the adversarial procedure and to evolve a new procedure which will make it possible for the poor and the weak to bring the necessary material before the court for the purpose of securing enforcement of their fundamental rights.

The courts shed off the laissez faire approach in the judicial process particularly where it involves a question of enforcement of the fundamental rights and forge new tools, devise new methods and adopt new strategies for the purpose of making fundamental rights meaningful for the large masses of the people. The language of Art. 32(2) is not restrictive and permits the court to adopt any procedure which it considers appropriate in the circumstances of a given case for enforcing the fundamental rights.

In *Santhal Pargana Antyadoya Ashram vs. State of Bihar & others (1987) supp. SCC 141* the court obtained a report of the committee appointed by the court, accepted the report and gave directions to release and rehabilitate the bonded labourers identified by the committee. The State Governments were directed to carry out the statutory obligations under the Bonded Labour System Act, 1976.

The judges have extended the meaning of 'life' in Article 21. It means 'not merely animal existence or continued drudgery through life but the finer graces of human civilization which makes life worth living.' See *Board of Trustees, Port of Bombay vs. UP (1983) 1 SCC 124*. In *Subhash Kumar vs. UP (1991) 1 SCC 598* the right to life is held to mean the right of enjoyment of pollution free water and air for full enjoyment of life.

Justice Y.V. Chandrachud in *Keshavananda Bharti vs. State of Kerala (1973) 4 SCC 225* at page 949 echoed the concern of the court towards weaker sections when he said:

> The Court is not chosen by the people and is not responsible in the sense in which the house of the people is. However, it will win for itself a permanent place in the hearts of the people and augment its moral authority if it can shift the focus of judicial review from the numerical concept of minority protection to the humanitarian concept of the protection of the weaker section of the people. It is really the poor, starved and mindless millions

who need the court's protection for securing to themselves the enjoyment of human rights. In the absence of an explicit mandate the court should abstain from striking down a constitutional amendment which makes an endeavour 'to wipe out every tear from every eye'.

Judicial Review

As regards the extraordinary apellate jurisdiction of the Supreme Court under Article 136 of the Constitution, it has been used as an almost a source of judicial power with apparently no limitation except for Armed Forces. The following observations of the Apex Court in *Dhakeshwari Cotton Mills vs. CIT AIR 1955 SC 65* show that the court was against frittering the special leave jurisdiction by any set formula or rule.

It is not possible to define with any precision the limitations on the exercise of the discretionary jurisdiction vested in the courts by the constitutional provision made in Article 136. The limitations, whatever they be, are implicit in the nature and character of the power itself. It being an exceptional and overriding power, naturally it has to be exercised sparingly and with caution and only in special and extraordinary situations. Beyond that it is not possible to fetter the exercise of this power by any set formula or rule.

It is Justice Krishna Iyer who will be always remembered as the Judge of the toiling masses of weaker sections of the society. He has been the champion of the underdog— 'the little man'—in securing him justice—social, economic and political. He never became a prisoner of dogmas but gave legal vitality to new approaches over the widest spectrum of social ills.

It would thus be seen that apex court judiciary has been continuously expanding the frontiers of fundamental rights and of natural justice. Some judges in particular have blazed new trails in constitutional interpretation.

A big reservoir of judicial power to control administrative action lies in Article 226 of the Constitution. Even when the fifty-second amendment inserted in Article 226 provided that the petition shall not be entertained if any other remedy for such redress is provided for by or under any other law did not seem to have produced any change in the attitude of the courts. If alternative remedy was illusory and not real and capable of giving such redress, the judges went ahead in providing relief. The judges have come forward to provide relief whenever they have found manifest injustice being done to the petitioner.

Expanding Governmental Activity

In India judicial review has been a constitutionally embraced concept and is the clear grant of basic law. The judiciary neither has a purse nor a sword. The fears of judicial fundamentalism or of a judicial autocracy are totally unfounded. The increasing judicialisation of political life is part of the popular demand of the modern era where state is required to fulfil its constitutional goals. The courts were earlier merely the interpreter of laws. The large scale public administration poses great challenges to the constitutional and political order. Justice William Douglas remarked:

> The bureaucracy of the modern Government is not only slow, lumbering and oppressive, (but also) it is omnipresent. Today's mounting bureaucracy both at the State and Federal levels promises to be suffocating and repressive unless it is put into the harness of procedural due process.... The sovereign of this nation is the people and not the bureaucracy.

The courts have stepped-in to make public administration more answerable and responsive in relation to individual constitutional rights. The judges have a duty to defend fundamental rights, the basic structure of the Constitution and the principles governing a democracy. The criticism against judiciary of being majoritarian is ill founded. The judicial review power is an essential part of the rule of law and constitutionalism.

A very important power wielded by the judiciary is the power to review decisions of public authorities. Most of the fundamental rights are available against the 'State' as defined under Article 12 of the Constitution. The decision of Justice P.N. Bhagwati in *R.D. Shetty vs. International Airport Authority of India AIR 1979 SC 1628* acted as a catalyst to judicial activism in an era of ever expanding governmental activities and proliferation of corporations. He adopted the functional test and observed:

...where a corporation is an instrumentality or agency of Government, it would, in the exercise of its power of discretion, be subject to the same constitutional or public law limitations as Government. The rule inhibiting arbitrary action by Government.... must apply equally where such corporation is dealing with the public, whether by way of giving jobs or entering into contracts or otherwise, and it cannot act arbitrarily and enter into relationship with any person it likes at its sweet will, but its action must be in conformity with some principle which meets the test of reason and relevance.

Judicial Restraint on Political Issues

The judges have consciously used self-restraint in relation to (a) political questions; (b) legislative powers; and (c) discretionary powers of the administration. For example, in *Keshavananda Bharti vs. State of Kerala AIR 1973 SC 1461 (2008-2009)* Justice Dwivedi observed:

Structural socio-political value choices involve a complex and complicated political process. This Court is hardly fitted for performing that function. In the absence of any explicit Constitutional norms and for want of complete evidence, the court's structural value choices will be largely subjective. Our personal predilections will unavoidably enter into the scale and give colour to our judgement. Subjectivism is calculated to undermine legal certainty, an essential element to the rule of law.

The judges have avoided, as far as possible, deciding political questions. In *S.R. Bommai vs. UOI (1994) 3 SCC 1* the Supreme Court examined the nature of President's power under Article 356 and the scope of judicial review. Justice Verma observed:

> Only cases which permit application of totally objective standards for deciding whether the constitutional machinery has failed, are amenable to judicial review and the remaining cases wherein there is any significant area of subjective satisfaction dependent on some imponderables or influences are not justiciable because there are no judicially manageable standards for resolving that controversy; and those cases are only subject to political scrutiny and correction.... The ultimate opinion formed in such cases, would be mostly a subjective political judgement. There are no judicially manageable standards for scrutinising such materials and resolving such a controversy. By its very nature such controversy cannot be justiciable.... These political decisions call for judicial hands off envisaging correction only by a subsequent electoral verdict, unless corrected earlier in Parliament.

Justice Ramaswamy advocated restraint in such situations and observed:

> Judicial review may be avoided on questions of purely political nature, though pure legal questions camouflaged by the political questions are always justiciable. The courts must have judicially manageable standards to decide a particular controversy. Justiciability on a subjective satisfaction conferred in the widest terms to the political coordinate executive branch created by the constitutional scheme itself is one of the considerations to be kept in view in exercising judicial review. There is an initial presumption that the acts have been regularly performed by the President.

It is, however, to be borne in mind that any legal question having political overtones should not be characterised a political question.

Even in relation to legislative powers, the judges have shown judicial self-restraint by the test of the presumption of the constitutionality when the validity of a statute is challenged by adopting the device of 'reading down'. In *K.R. Lakshmanan vs. T.N. (1996) 2 SCC 226* the court observed:

> It is true that the presumption is in favour of the constitutionality of a legislative enactment and it is to be presumed that a legislature understands and appreciates the needs of its own people, but when on the face of the Statute there is no classification and no attempt has been made to select an individual with reference to any differentiating attributes peculiar to that individual and not possessed by others, the presumption is of no assistance to the state.

Law and Justice

The function of judges is to deliver justice according to law. It is this basic test that has to be kept in mind while judging the judges. The relationship between law and justice has been beautifully described by Justice Iyer, thus:

> Law is a means to an end and justice is that end. But in actuality, law and justice are distant neighbours; sometimes even strange hostiles. If law shoots down justice, the people shoot down law and lawlessness paralyses development, disrupts order and retards progress. This is the current scene.

One should also recall the prophetic warning sounded by the greater thinker Robert Ingersoll:

> A government founded upon anything except liberty and justice cannot stand. All the wrecks on either side of the stream of time, all the wrecks of the great cities, all the nations that have passed away — all are a warning that no nation founded upon injustice can stand. From the sand shrouded Egypt, from the marble wilderness of Athens and from every fallen, crumbling stone of the once mighty Rome, comes a wail as it were, the cry that no nation founded upon injustice can permanently stand.

Daniel Webstar said a century and a half ago:

> Justice Sir, is the greatest interest of man on earth. It is the ligament which holds civilised beings and civilised nations together. Wherever her temple stands, and so long as it is duly honoured there is a foundation for social security, general happiness and the improvement and progress of our race. And whoever labours on the edifice with usefulness and distinction, whoever clears its foundations, strengthens its pillars, adorns its entablatures or contributes to raise its august dome still higher in the skies, connects himself in name and fame and character with that which is and must be as durable as the frame of human society.

The almost collapse of responsible government by the executive, the courts were duty bound to come forward and fail not the people of this country. The judges have been anxious to ensure that social change in consonance with the philosophy of the constitution takes place without impediments from other branches of the government.

Role of the Judges

The founding fathers made the legislature trustees of the powers reposed in them and guardians of the peoples' liberties. The judiciary was to be an auxiliary check on the powers of the state organisations when in legislative bodies, the legislative business is not seriously transacted and there is bureaucratic apathy to the problems of the people, the void is sought to be filled in by resort to courts. The enlightened, independent judiciary is vital for the throbbing and growing democracy. The independence of the judiciary is rightly regarded as the key principle of the constitution. In this connection Lord Denning has aptly described the role of judges:

> It is the role of the Judges in developing the law. Many of the Judges have said that they do not make law. They only interpret it. This is an illusion which they have fostered. But it is a notion which is now being discarded everywhere. Every new decision—on every new

situation—is a development of the law. Law does not stand still. It moves continually. Once this is recognised, then the task of the Judge is put on a higher plane. He must consciously seek to mould the law so as to serve the needs of the time. He must not be a mere mechanic, a mere working mason, laying brick on brick, without thought to the overall design. He must be an architect—thinking of the structure as a whole—building for society a system of law which is strong, durable and just. It is on his work that civilised society itself depends.

Lord Mac Millan observed:

It is thus clear that the judiciary are constantly confronted with the necessity of making a choice between the doctrine of the law which they are to hold applicable to a particular case, and the choice which they make in the particular instance results inevitably in the expansion of restriction of the doctrine applied or rejected. It is at this point that what may, I think, quite properly be called ethical considerations operate and ought to operate. I hope I shall be acquitted of any suggestion that judges should allow themselves to be swayed by sentiment to wrest the law, and I should deprecate as strongly as any the admission of the motives of the social reformer into the counsels of the Bench. I am no friend of that spurious kind of equity which Lord Bromwell robustly denounces as consisting in 'A disregard of general principles and general rules in the endeavour to do justice more or less fanciful in particular cases.' Other eminent judges in equally vigorous language, to which I am prepared to subscribe, have condemned the impropriety of allowing other than purely legal considerations to influence the decisions of the courts. But when, as happens from time to time, the law itself presents a choice, and when it is a question whether one or other principle is to be applied, then it seems to me that it is impossible as it is undesirable, that the decision should not have regard to the ethical motive of promoting justice.

Earl Warren, the great Chief Justice of the United States stressed the importance of the judicial function by observing:

Our judges are not monks or scientists, but participants in the living stream of our national life, steering the law between the dangers of rigidity on the one hand and of formlessness on the other. Our system faces no theoretical dilemma but a single continuous problem; how to apply to everchanging conditions the never-changing principles of freedom.

The society has great expectations from the judges. Felix Frankfurter puts it thus:

A judge should be compounded of the faculties that are demanded of the historian and the philosopher and the prophet. The last demand upon him—to make some forecast of the consequences of his action—is perhaps the heaviest. To pierce the curtain of the future, to give shape and visage to mysteries still in the womb of time, is the gift of the imagination. It requires poetic sensibilities with which judges are rarely endowed and which their education does not normally develop. These judges must have something of the creative artist in them; they must have antennae registering feeling and judgement beyond logical, let alone quantitative, proof.

Professor Pannick in his book titled *Judges* has observed:

Judges do not have an easy job. They repeatedly do what the rest of us seek to avoid; make decisions.

He further added:

Judges are mortals but they are asked to perform a function that is utterly divine.

Justice Medina in 'The Judge and his God; We are not the Masters' [38 ABAJ 661, 662-663 (1952)] observed:

I do not see why a judge should be ashamed to say that he prays for divine guidance and for strength to do his duty. Indeed there came a time.... when I did the most sincere and the most fervent praying that I ever did in my life.

I suddenly found myself in the midst of the trial of the communists. It took me a long time to realise what they were trying to do to me. But as I got weaker and weaker, and found the burden difficult to bear, I sought strength from the one source that never fails.... my unguided will alone and such self-control as I possess were unequal to the test.

Society's Expectations and Judges

The distinct nature of the duties that a judge is called upon to discharge, the society's expectations of the conduct of the judge, the occupational hazards to which he is exposed and of the need to keep judges above their essential wants has been illustrated well by David Pannick in his above referred book which is not only true in the context of English judges but equally if not more to our judges. The following observations have been quoted with approval by the Apex Court in All India Judges Association case:

The reasons which judges must give to justify their decisions can be gnawed over at their leisure by the teams of lawyers trained (and generously paid) to extract for the purpose of an appeal, every morsel of error.... The judge has the burden of resolving, day after day and week after week, a long succession of issues, each one of which occupies the professor-critic for months and even years of specialized study.

The English judge has no clerks or assistants to research or write his judgements. The barristers who argue the case before him will 'vary much in their ability'. Sometimes they help but often they may be hindrance to the just determination of the issues.

The judge has burdensome responsibilities to discharge. He has power over the lives and livelihood of all those who enter his court.... His decisions may well affect the interests of individuals and groups who are not present or represented in court. If he is not careful, the judge may precipitate a civil war... or he may accelerate a revolution.... He may accidentally cause a peaceful but fundamental change in the political complexion of the country.

Judges today face tribulations as well as trials not contemplated by their predecessors.... Parliament has recognised the pressures of the job by providing that before the Lord Chancellor recommends anyone to the Queen for appointment to Circuit Bench, the Lord Chancellor shall take steps to satisfy himself that the person's health is satisfactory.... This seems essential in the light of the reminiscences of Lord Roskill as to the mental strain which the job can impose.... Lord Roskill added that in his experience, 'the workload is intolerable; seven days a week, 14 hours a day....'

Only in England could the vocation of the judge be described as 'something like a priesthood' or 'analogous to the Royal Family', requiring practitioners to 'seclude themselves' in various ways....

In England we expect the judge to adopt a respectable lifestyle, free from any hint of the unusual, let alone the deviant.

In 1950, a Member of Parliament.... recommended an even greater degree of judicial isolation.... So effective is the isolation of our judiciary that the personalities and characteristics of our judges are unknown to laymen....

The English judge ensures in a quiet but effective manner that his pay accords with his status. He avoids the public display of militancy... Judge Rank Coffin of the US Court of Appeals complained in 1985 about the inadequacy of 'compensation' for judges. In the previous few years, he lamented, judicial salaries had become so insufficient that only the mediocre or the wealthy would henceforth be willing to take judicial appointments. Perhaps disappointing pay levels help to explain why a clinical psychologist was helping judges in Massachusetts to cope with stress.... He also provided counselling to enable the retired judge 'to maintain self-esteem'....

He (judge) is a symbol of that strange mixture of reality and illusion, democracy and privilege, humbug and decency, the subtle network of compromises, by which the nation keeps itself in its familiar shape.

The qualities desired of a judge can be simply state; 'that if he be a good one and he be thought to be so.' Such credentials are not easily acquired. The judge needs to have 'the strength to put an end to injustice' and 'the faculties that are demanded of the historian and the philosopher and the prophet'.

It is unlikely that men and women will ever cease to wound, cheat, and damage each other. There will always be a need for judges to resolve their disputes in an orderly manner. As people grow ever less willing to accept unreservedly the demands of authority, the judiciary, like other public institutions, will be subjected a growing amount of critical analysis. The way in which 'Judge and Co.' is run is a matter of public debate.

The Law Commission in its 14th Report said:

If the public is to give profound respect to the judges, the judges should by their conduct try and observe it; not by word or deed should they give cause for the people that they do not deserve the pedestal on which we expect the public to place them. It appears to us that not only for the performance of his duties but outside the Court as well a Judge has to maintain an aloofness amounting almost to self-imposed isolation.

The Commission quoted Sir Winston Churchill who had said:

A form of life and conduct far more severe and restricted than that of ordinary people is required from judges and though unwritten has been most strictly observed. They are at once privileged and restricted; they have to present a continuous aspect of dignity and conduct.

The Apex Court further observed in the said case:

These prescriptions for a Judicial Officer, therefore, result in a restricted life. Austerity is a quality to be practised by every Judge—personally as also in his public functioning. This necessarily gives rise to a situation where the Judge must have patience, perseverance and painstaking habits. In order that a Judge may be able to put in these aspects into his public functioning, it is absolutely necessary that the Judge enjoys freedom from personal worries. A reasonable salary, appropriate allowances and manageable living conditions are, therefore, required to be provided.

Greater emphasis has been placed on the qualities of a trial judge by observing:

The trial Judge is the kingpin in the hierarchical system of administration of Justice. He directly comes in contact with the litigant during the proceedings in Court. On him lies the responsibility of building up of the case appropriately and on his understanding of the matter the cause of justice is first answered. The personality, knowledge, judicial restraint, capacity to maintain dignity are the additional aspects which go into making the Court's functioning successful.

As members of the judiciary, they exercise the sovereign judicial power of the State. They are holders of public offices in the same way as the members of the council of ministers and the members of the legislature. When it is said that in a democracy such as ours, the executive, the legislature and the judiciary constitute the three pillars of the State, what is intended to be conveyed is that the three essential functions of the State are entrusted to the three organs of the State and each one of them in turn represents the authority of the State. However, those who exercise the State power are the ministers, the legislatures and the Judges, and not the members of their staff who implement or assist in implementing their decisions. The council of ministers or the political executive is different from the secretarial staff or the administrative executive which carries out the directions of the political executive. Similarly, the legislators are different from the legislative staff. So also the Judges from the judicial staff. The parity is between the political executive, the legislators and the Judges and not between the Judges and the administrative executive. In some democracies like the USA, members of some State judiciaries are elected as much as the members of the legislature and the heads of the State. The Judges, at whatever level they may be, represent the State and its authority unlike the administrative executive or the members of the other services. The members of the other services, therefore, cannot be placed on par with the members of the judiciary, either constitutionally or functionally.

This distinction between the Judges and the members of the other services has to be constantly kept in mind for yet another important reason. Judicial independence cannot be secured by making mere solemn proclamations about it. It has to be secured both in substance and in practice. It is trite to say that those who are in want cannot be free. Self-reliance is the foundation of independence of the judiciary and no price is too heavy to secure it. To keep the Judges in want of the essential accountrements and thus to impede them in the proper discharge of their duties is to impair and whittle away justice itself.

Qualities of Judges

Speedy and satisfactory disposal of cases depends on competence and personality of judges. The judges selected should be men of character and integrity. They should be well-versed in Law and Jurisprudence.

Shukraniti (ch. IV-5-15-18) says:

व्यवहारविदः प्राज्ञा वृतशील गुणान्विताः।
रिपो नित्रे समा ये च धर्मज्ञास्सत्य वदिनः।।

निरालसा जित क्रोध काम लोभः प्रियंवदा।
राज्ञा नियोजित व्यास्ते सम्यास्सर्वासु जातिषु।।

"One who is well-versed in civil and criminal law and procedure, sprightful, of sterling character, impartial towards friends and foes, of Dharma abiding nature, truthful, ever active and who has established control over anger, desire and greed and pleasant in speech and demeanour should be appointed a judge."

Trial judges have to take care that innocents are not punished and an offender should not go unpunished.

Manusmriti says:

पिताचार्य सुद्धन्माता भार्या पुत्रः पुरोहिताः।
नादण्डयो नाम राक्षौस्ति य स्वधर्मे न तिष्ठिति।।

"The King should not leave an offender unpunished, whatever may be his relationship with him. Neither father, nor a teacher, nor a friend, nor mother, nor wife, nor a son, nor a domestic priest should go unpunished for the offence committed."

Our ancient scriptures prescribe the qualification and duties of a judge. Atrismriti (28) says:

दुष्टस्य दण्डः सुजनस्य पूजा।
न्यायेन कोषस्य च संप्रवृद्धि।।

अपक्षपातो र्थिषु राष्ट्ररक्षा।
पच्चैव यज्ञाः कथिता नृपाणाम।।

"To punish the wicked, to protect the good, to enrich the treasury (exchequer) by just methods, to render justice impartially to the litigants and to protect the kingdom— these are the five yagnas (selfless duties) to be performed by a King (the State)"

In Shukraniti (ch-V-14-15) it is stated:

पक्षपाताधिरोपस्य कारणानि च पच्च वै।
रागलोभभयद्वेषा वादिनोश्च रहरश्रुतिः।।

"There are five causes which give rise to the charge of partiality (against the judges). They are (i) *Raga* (affection in favour of a party); (ii) *Lobha* (greed); (iii) *Bhaya* (fear); (iv) *Dwesha* (ill will against a party); and (v) *Vadinoscha Rahashruthi* (the judge meeting and hearing a party to a case secretly)."

Narada Smriti says:

यात्यचोरोपिचोरत्वं चोरश्चायात्य चोरताम।
अचोश्चोरता प्राप्तो माण्डव्यो व्यवहारतः।।

"One who has not committed theft or robbery may be found guilty of that offence. An actual thief or robber on the other hand may be acquitted of the charge. Mandavya (an ascetic who was innocent) was tried and declared to be guilty — hence judges must be extremely careful in recording findings."

Judicial Independence

Our judiciary comprises a broad range of independent and fair-minded people with a considerable variety of attitudes and opinions. Judiciary is now recruited from the legal profession at all levels. The lowest judiciary is recruited from practising advocates and the district judiciary is further strengthened by induction from the bar in a certain proportion.

The government is intending to revert to pre-1993 position when judicial appointments were the prerogative of the executive. The nine-judges' bench on October 6, 1993 gave full power to the judiciary over judicial appointments.

There has been extremely low credibility of both the executive and the legislature. It was judiciary alone which was held in high esteem. The corruption cases, the various scams involving politicians marred their public image. There have been attempts to gag the judiciary because of several cases pending against political personalities. There is also demand for setting up a National Judicial Commission. This is, in fact, not a new idea. The Constitution (67th amendment) Bill, 1990 was introduced by the then government on May 18, 1990 empowering the President to constitute a high level judicial commission for making recommendations for the appointment of judges of the superior judiciary. The Bill lapsed as the 9th Lok Sabha was dissolved.

It is absolutely vital for the health of the nation that independence of the judiciary at all levels is maintained and respected. No one either within the judiciary or outside can legally influence a judge in the discharge of his judicial functions. It is of vital importance that judges must be true to the judicial oath and no one must be allowed to interfere with that. The judge must be able to give judgement according to the laws of the land without fear or favour, affection or ill will. The judge has a right to decide for or against the executive in all its branches according to the merits of the case without any influence whatever from the executive except in the form of submissions put before the judge in accordance with the principles of natural justice. Within the judiciary no other judge, however, superior or eminent, is entitled to tell the judge what to do. This does not mean that judges are not bound by judicial discipline. Every judge has to give due regard to the judgements which are binding on him. Judicial independence is a key principle and must be preserved.

Our judges have that sense of justice which Roscopound explained as the totality of values as to human relations intuitively recognised through collective expressive and what David Miller said by defining justice 'to each according to his right, desert and need'.

The criticism of the judiciary being overactive and usurping the powers of the other State organisations is unfounded. The courts do not grab at ungranted jurisdiction but at the same time the judiciary should neither shrink from the exercise of that which is conferred upon it. What is being described as judicial activism is, in fact, judicial pragmatism and judicial statesmanship.

6

LAW AS CONTEMPT OF JUSTICE

V.N. Narayanan

No profession is so insular and so zealous in guarding and exercising its powers with the widest latitude in interpreting its scope and extent as the judiciary. And no other class of powerful people are so allergic to both self-regulation and scrutiny by external agencies as the judges. The higher judiciary, all over the world, is the only institution that treats itself as accountable only to itself. The safeguard for nations in allowing this unaccountability primarily lay in the generally high standards set by judges, both in terms of professional excellence and personal integrity.

In an atmosphere of declining morals and decaying institutions of democracy, the judicial insularity turns into judicial activism and later, into judicial arrogance. The former phenomenon begins as a beneficent movement towards vesting the courts with the power to interpret the law not in terms of the letter of the law but in terms of the social and political reality of law's inadequacy and impotence. At this stage the judiciary takes up cases that are not only socially relevant but also provide scope for interpreting the law as a pro-people instrument of justice relying on the spirit of the law rather than the letter.

At the next stage, activism discovers that its pro-people judgments do not have the desired effect because the government agencies do not implement the verdicts. Issuing orders to the administration produce routine bureaucratic replies and inordinately delayed and invariably evasive. Soon the judiciary discovers that there are large gaping holes in the institutions of democracy which had rendered both government and Parliament incapable of enforcing the laws they had got passed and are obligated to enforce.

The judiciary abhors a vacuum as much as nature does; more so if it happens to be a power vacuum. So the pro-people straying from the letter of the law converts itself into occupying the space left vacant by an ignorant parliament and an impotent government. Instead of interpreting the law and the Constitution, the courts start issuing executive orders— "evolve civil code," fix quotas, "evict residents", "clear garbage", "supply food to hostages" and fix the calorie content of the food thus supplied, and so on. From putting the government and legislatures in their places, the judiciary itself moves into their place without any sanction except its own.

That leads us into the second consequence—judicial autocracy. The black-robed whistle-blowers get so used to blowing the whistle at everybody from the Prime Minister and legislators to bureaucrats, election commissioners, industrialists and editors that they cannot visualise the possibility of the whistle being blown at them. Conscious of their power and aware of the fact that they are not delivering judgments in cases but addressing a national audience on vital issues of governance and legislation have made them see themselves in convex mirror images. As the judge in the Gilbert and Sullivan opera says...

The law is the true embodiment
Of everything that's excellent
It has no kind of fault or flaw,
And, I, my lords, embody the law.

Perhaps the one law which confers on judges at all levels an enormous amount of power is the Contempt of Courts. Strangely enough this is one law which goes against the very basis of jurisprudence in civilised societies. It is also the one law which makes the prosecutor the judge in his own case. It is also the only law which seeks to set the judges apart from the rest of the citizenry in society and polity. All over the world, the judicial establishment has recognised this anomalous situation and rectified it by virtually desisting from invoking this archaic law to emphasise the awful majesty of Law. However, in India, the contempt law is a routine judicial bludgeon brandished before a questioning citizen to beat him to silent obeisance to the court.

Of course, the justification for this extraordinary power has been that the judiciary is an institution for serving the people and safeguarding the rights of the people and upholding the Constitution and not for its own aggrandisement. In a sense even a politician vying for power can say that. Criticism of every public institution is vital as a check on power and, for precisely that reason, criticism of the judges and judicial conduct must be recognised as an essential part of civil society.

Why does the law of Contempt, not accept the belief of John Stuart Mill that we must allow even erroneous opinions to be expressed in the hope that the correct ones may become more firmly established by what may be called a dialectical process of struggle with wrong ones?

Does the law of Contempt, not cock a snook at Milton who said:

> Though all the winds of doctrine were let loose to play upon the earth, so Truth be in the field, we do injuriously by licensing and prohibiting her misdoubt her strength. Let her and Falsehood grapple; whoever knew Truth put to the worse, in a free and open encounter?

If the political philosophers and historians have taught us that intellectual advances made by our civilizations would have been impossible without freedom of speech and expression, can the opposite hold true, in the case of the Judiciary? If political democracy is based on the assumption that freedom must be jealously guarded, can the Judiciary justify banishing freedom of expression, when it comes to its own conduct and functioning? Would the Judiciary reverse a democrat's faith of *Voltaire,* when he told an adversary in arguments:

> I do not agree with a word of what you say, but I will defend to death, your right to say it.

If freedom of the Press is the Art of the Covenant of Democracy and if public criticism is essential to the working of its institutions, can the Judiciary remain a forbidden territory from public criticism?

The Judiciary in India, which has championed the human freedom of thought and expression and has believed that intellectual atrophy affects every society which denies this freedom in howsoever subtle a form, cannot deprive itself of the same medicine. Some of the most liberal and enlightened Judges of the Supreme Court of India, have upheld these values while dealing with allegations of unfair criticism of their actions. Says Justice Krishna Iyer, in the case of In *Re S. Mulgaokar:*

> Indeed, to criticise a Judge fairly albeit fiercely, is no crime, but a necessary right, twice blessed in a democracy. For it blesseth him that gives and him that takes. Where freedom of expression fairly exercised, serves public interest in reasonable measure, public justice cannot gag it or manacle it, constitutionally speaking.

Justice Krishna Iyer quotes Lord Denning's observations in *Regina vs. Metropolitan Police Commissioner.:*

> Let me say at once that we will never use this jurisdiction as means to uphold our own dignity. That must rest on surer foundations. Nor will we use it, to suppress those who speak against us. We do not fear criticism nor do we resent it, for there is something far more important at stake. It is no less than freedom of speech itself.

Chief Justice Gajendragadkar, in the case of Shri Baradakanta Mishra said:

> Even so, if Judges have frailties, after all, they are humans and they need to be corrected by independent criticism. If the Judicature has serious shortcomings which demand systematic correction through socially oriented reforms initiated through constructive criticism, the contempt power should not be an interdict. Creative Legal Journalism and active statesmanship for Judicial reform cannot be jeopardised by undefined apprehension of contempt action.

The Indian Law has avoided confusion between the personal protection of a libelled Judge and prevention of obstruction of public justice. Scandalising the Court means hostile criticism of the Judge as Judge; any personal attack upon him, unconnected with the office he holds, is dealt with under the ordinary rules of slander and libel. The Supreme Court of India, thus approved the observations of the Privy Council, made in the case of Bahamas Islands that the references to the Chief Justice, in the Guardian, were highly sarcastic, yet since they did not refer to the Chief Justice in his official as opposed to personal capacity, they did not constitute contempt.

While the Indian Courts have consistently advised against Judges being hypersensitive, even when criticism of them oversteps the limits, yet they continue to deflate vulgar denunciations of the Judiciary.

With regard to the role of the Fourth Estate, the Indian Law regards it as an indispensable intermediary between the State and the people and a necessary instrumentality for strengthening the forces of democracy. The Courts have tended to give freeplay, within responsible limits, to the media.

The law, however, is sufficiently flexible and continues to be subjective and gets moulded, according to the philosophy and temper of the Judge(s) concerned. There is a serious school of thought that the power of contempt for scandalising the Court, needs to be legislatively circumscribed, to remove the vague element of fear, that prevails in the minds of public men, journalists and commentators. That fear arises not from the force of the law but from the attitude of judges. Stretched to the limits, the contempt law is contemptible... It commits the sin of contempt on justice.

7

APPOINTMENT OF JUDGES AND SYSTEMATIC CHANGES IN JUDICIAL SYSTEM

Sitaram Yechury

This is a subject of such importance which is not only confined to the judiciary or to the judicial system in our country but also to the existence of democracy and to the institution of democracy as a whole because of the administration of Justice. And, this is something which we firmly believe in as one of the strongest pillars of democracy. The judiciary by administration of justice not only does fairness and justice to the people in a democracy but also instills a sense of confidence and acts as a conscience that strengths democracy. So any talk of lack of confidence in the Judiciary or undermining the Judiciary and its functioning has an impact that goes beyond the system of administration of Justice. It affects the system of democracy as a whole and therefore it is in the interest of everyone to overcome some of the problems or some of the potential problems that are likely to occur. We are at the time in India where some of these problems and the potential problems are seeking themselves out and begging to be noticed so that we can bring in certain corrections.

'Judging the Judges' is not merely the question of the fairness of the Judiciary. There are three basic and important areas to which we should pay attention today. The first one is on the question of the fairness of the judiciary in terms of the appointment of the authorities of the judiciary, particularly at the highest level. This is one area which needs to be discussed. The second is the question of "Justice delayed is Justice virtually denied." And the delay that we are facing in our system today with thousands of cases pending is indeed gigantic. This is something which will have to be tackled. The third area is what today, has become very fashionable for everybody to talk about is Judicial Activism. All of us should work together in solving some of these problems.

The first one is the question of the entire appointment of the structure of the Judiciary in our country. This is a very important matter that we must discuss amongst ourselves frankly at the outset, with the highest respect that we all have for the judiciary. It is not the integrity of the Judges that is being questioned. But it is the infallibility of the individuals that is under question. In a democracy we have to evolve a system where the fallibility of individuals can be corrected without questioning or doubting their integrity. And unless we are able to make a reasoned and a scientific separation of these two issues, I think the emotive element will not be separated which often has been causing problems when it comes to the question of appointment of judges at the highest level or the functioning of the Judiciary itself. I would suggest the constitution of a National Judicial Commission with appropriate amendments to the Constitution where the appointment of the Judges are not to be confined only to the Executive or the Chief Executive and the Chief Justice as it often happens in practice in many of the states particularly or even at the higher level. It is not a matter that should be decided only by a set of individuals holding office but it should be decided by a collegium or let us say by an Electoral College or by a Commission which is multi-member and at the same time accountable to the authority that sets up this Commission namely the Constitution of India, such an authority will be a combination of all the three pillars of our democracy. So this, is not a rigid position that is not open to any discussion. But, the essential principle behind this entire thing is that the appointment of the judges will have to be made not by a single authority or a set of individuals but by a body, an institutional body that is accountable to the people and at the same time also responsible for strengthening democracy. We are suggesting this keeping in mind the disputed principle of democracy that the larger the number of people involved in taking a decision, the more balanced will be the decision that is taken. This Judicial Commission, therefore, will have to be multi-member one apart from being accountable. Now this is as far as the first point is concerned. Never did anyone think that you could have a Judge of the Supreme Court, an honourable Judge of the Supreme Court against whom an impeachment motion was brought before the Parliament on grounds of corruption. Now, this is something that saddens one's heart. We do not want such a thing to happen. It's not that we didn't envisage such a possibility. If so this provision for impeachment would not been there at all. But on corruption charges! And you have now an enquiry of an ex-judge of the High Court in Calcutta. He is being questioned about the disproportionate assets acquired during his time as a judge. Now these are things which should concern all of us. Let us forget for the time being, to which end of the political spectrum we belong to. This is not an issue for scoring points but this is eating into the very vitals of this very system that each one of us is really interested in strengthening. Now taking this into account the appointing authority assumes great importance.

The question of transfer of Judges has also come under a lot of cloud and a lot of comments are taking place all over. All this should be looked into by a National Judicial Commission which with proper amendments of Constitution can be brought about.

Regarding the 2nd issue—the question of these large number of cases that are still pending. This is actually something that many bequeath to the next generation—a litigation.

Political parties have been accustomed to adding one paragrah in their political manifestos saying that clearing of all pending cases will be done at the earliest etc. The United Front has done it in the Common Minimum Programme that we have all drafted but when it actually comes to the mechanics of how you are going about it, problem comes. It is not merely a question of inadequate number of Judges. There is a lot of review to be done when restructuring and the fixing of our system that will have to be done where cases will have to be disposed of within a time limit. It cannot be left to the individual choices and opinions of individual judges in the present situation today. There has to be a certain time limit that will have to be fixed. Now that very legitimately can be argued of interference in the process of administration of Justice. But I think a balance has to be struck somewhere. In the name of proper administration of Justice, delay in administering Justice cannot be allowed. This is where I think collectively along with the Judiciary, the Executive and the Legislature, all three will have to act together and bring about these correctives. We had promised in the Common Minimum Programme of the United Front that pending cases will all be cleared within three years. But that is a wish, it is not something that we actually think is feasible. We would like them all to be cleared but, we have just not been able to come up with anything concrete to suggest that how it can be done. A job of clearing such a stupendous backlog is there. Definitely on this some mechanisms will have to be formulated in terms of fixing the time limit for the types of cases that will have to be put up before the courts.

The third issue is the fashionable term, of judicial activism. This is an issue which by the very nature of the issue one will have to be a little careful with the type of talking one has to do. If there's one thing that virtually terrifies any politician in our country it is this contempt of court because you really do not know when you open your mouth and say what which can have a fine slapped on you. A fine was slapped on E.M.S. Namboodripad for a perfectly justified political comment that he had made at that point of time. I think it is necessary to recollect the age-old dictum that in a democracy respect must be commanded and not demanded. And Judiciary will have to set the example in a judicious manner in this respect. On the question of judicial activism there are in my opinion two developments that are taking place today. Currently, the judiciary, at various levels, is displaying a tremendous degree of vigilance and initiative in ensuring that Justice is brought about and the culprits are booked, particularly in a large number of cases of corruption that involves high profited individuals. Their role here is laudatory in ensuring that such actions and decisions are being taken. The process is also getting speeded up. At the same time, there is also a certain fear that many of us share that they are transgressing the boundaries of Judiciary and entering the realm of the Executive and the Legislature. This is reflected in many of the decisions and in many of the judgements that they are pronouncing. For obvious reasons I do not want to go into individual cases to illustrate the point. This, however, is not a good reflection of our system when you have the Supreme Court deciding on the quantum of fees that will be imposed by Dental Colleges in Karnataka. Now these are not matters for the Judiciary. But the question is that there are areas where such transgression is taking place. And the transgression of one arm of democracy over the authority of the other arm is the most unhealthy thing to happen in the functioning of a democracy. Now this is being made possible in today's situation because of the inability or the ineffectivity of the Executive in implementing the Rule of the Land. And this is the root cause of this entire problem. If the Executive and the Legislature were able to tackle the problems that were there, the need of the judiciary to step in would not have arisen at all. But the need for the Judiciary to step in having arisen cannot be the alibi or the plea for the Judiciary to transgress the boundaries of the other arms. What is required is a healthy admixture of the clear definitions which our Constitution does among the three pillars of our democracy. But at the same time, to ensure that none of these transgress on the other, like there is no Executive's interference in the judicial process or there is no transgressing of the Judiciary in the tasks of the Executive. Now these are some things that we will have to be brought forward in our country today and in that direction, a National Debate particularly is to be initiated. And on those lines a large number of members of the bar have already taken some initiative. Some of them have made some suggestions. Much thinking has also gone into it and it will be our endeavour to try and ensure and hopefully make others also to agree to this sort of a proposal that we should have a National Judicial Commission that would be able to take care of at least some, if not all of the problems that fall within the ambit of 'Judging the Judges'. And finally, I would only like to submit that at least not for a moment should we lose sight of the fact that in today's conditions. In India even to the most illiterate, even to the most backward of the Indian people if there is any one arbiter of Justice that is there in our country, it is our Kacheri, it is our courts and it is our Judiciary. There is a tremendous degree of faith that still is there in the people in this institution and God forbid if this faith also goes like it has gone to some degree and extent in some other institutions of our country, then the entire foundations of democracy in our country can really not be protected. Unless some of these problems are tackled with urgency we may end up in actually cutting the branch on which we are sitting not merely for the Judiciary but for the system as a whole. That is why these things will have to be addressed with great urgency. These are some of the issues, that will have to be addressed with great urgency.

8

DECENTRALISATION OFJUDICIAL SYSTEM AND REFORM OF JUDICIAL PROCEDURAL NEEDED TO CURB CORRUPTION OTHERWISE LEAVE IT TO JUDICIAL CONSCIENCE

Syed Shahabuddin

Under the Constitution the Judiciary is to act as the watchdog both of the Legislature and the Executive. It has the power to review the constitutionality of the laws enacted by the legislatures as well as to sit on judgement on the legality of the acts of omission and commission by the Executive, political and permanent.

When the democratic order is being eroded, the Judiciary is being seen increasingly as the rampart of the citadel of democracy. Indeed when both the legislature and the executive have lost their status and credibility in the public eye and the esteem that they once commanded, the Judiciary is looked upon as the last hope of the system, as the ultimate bulwark against corruption, against oppression and misuse of power and authority, as the ultimate check on the arbitrariness of those who wield power and the whims and fancies of those who are prepared to play with the Constitution to suit their political purposes.

But the judges are human beings. They are the products of the society which nurtures them genetically and socially, they have much in common with the members of the Executive and the Legislature. They suffer from the same failings, frailties and shortcomings. From the same bias and prejudice and the same ills and vices, because springing from the same society they cannot be immunised against the social malaise, once it becomes rampant.

This is not to say that there are no judges of integrity. They are some who would not allow a fly to rest on their nose, who would in utter disdain refuse any favour from the Government, who hear cases and not parties, who do not care for promotions or transfers or elevations, who lead a simple life, live like hermits, distancing themselves from the environment as far as possible, protecting themselves from the ill-wind which blows across the land. As Saghir Ahmad and G.B. Pattanaik, JJ. recently observed "Judges have to live and behave like "hermits" who have no desire or aspiration, having shed it through penance. Their mission is to supply light and not heat (AIR 1998 SC 1079)". But relatively speaking, such judges are few. The fact, therefore, is that the standards of probity have gone down and the fear of being hauled up for contempt alone cannot conceal what goes on or any longer silence the critics.

When the cancer of corruption has eaten into the vitals of the nation, when it is not only taken for granted but socially accepted and even rationalised as the key to development, it is not surprising if the corridors of justice are today echoing and resounding with whispers about contacts, influences, friendly tips and manipulations which are reflected in the composition of the benches, in the pace of hearing, in the exercise of discretionary authority by the judges and the deliberate delay, sometimes, in the pronouncements of judgement even after the hearing is over.

Our judicial system is today collapsing under the weight of arrears, though much was done by the former Chief Justice A.M. Ahmadi to reduce the load. If justice delayed is justice denied, delay invariably leads to corruption. The cases linger on for years. In the normal course a case may not be taken up for years. Even politically important case may gather dust.

The judiciary is generally perceived to be mute to pleas for preferential treatment, imperturbable in the face of urgency, certainly not taken to sudden bouts of activity. Therefore, it is surprising that sometimes it suddenly seems to come to life and act with a sense of urgency. Petitions are heard outside office hours, even on closed holiday, in order to dispense justice. The people of India should have cheered such dynamism, even though occasional, but for the fact that the attention is highly selective and gives rise to serious misgivings about motives or linkages between the judges, the lawyers and the parties concerned.

Since the Government is the plaintiff or the defendant in most of the cases before the higher judiciary, one may imagine that the Supreme Court and the High Court judges shall deliberately maintain discreet distance from the Government. But the present system makes them dependent on the legislature and the executive even for basic facilities, not to speak of the terms and conditions of service. The legislature determines their emoluments, the executive provides the housing and all that goes with it. The Executive plays a part not only in their recruitment but in their posting and transfer which is often an instrument in the hands of the Executive to harass. The Executive also tries to oblige the judges with a flat here, a plot there, a chairmanship after retirement and now even Governorship has been added to the list. That a judge on retirement may take to politics and be elected to a legislature and even become a Minister if he has the good sense to choose the right party at the right time. But this is his right as a citizen and therefore clearly permissible in any democracy. Though one wonders how many retired judges have entered the British Parliament or the US Congress on retirement.

Like ordinary mortals, following the example set by the politicians and the bureaucrats some judges also take care of their progeny to give them a head start in life. Blood relatives are technically barred from appearing before the judges but they are not before the other judges in the same High Court which leaves enough room for the game of reciprocity to merrily go on.

Under the existing system, the higher judiciary is basically a child of political patronage and, therefore, of calculated favouritism and all that it implies. The appointment is shrouded in mystery and, to say the least, far from transparent. Once raised to the bench, with or without merit, a judge of the High Court proceeds along the well-trodden path to become the Chief Justice of the High Court and, if he is lucky, to be elevated to the Supreme Court. If age is on his side he may retire as the Chief Justice. As in the higher bureaucracy once an officer is promoted to the selection grade all he is to do is to follow the path of least resistance, to float, to reach places. The system provides no incentives for excellence.

The strict interpretation of the law of contempt covers many a chink in the armour of a vulnerable judiciary. Indeed, contempt proceedings overawes the public, in general, the litigants in particular, and even the advocates shy into acquiescence and submission. What is not covered by the fear of being hauled up for contempt is taken care of by the existential compulsions or the human weakness, to be on the right side of the institution and of the person who is in authority, particular in a country which, by and large retains its feudal ethos. Who knows when next you may become a litigant and what is more the litigation may drag on for ages? One has to be courageous indeed to take on an institution like the judiciary!

Who will judge the judges? Certainly the Legislature or the Executive are in no position to speak to the Judiciary from a high moral ground. The people! But the people have no say. They exercise a theoretical control but passing through many levels, up or down, it is not practical unless the judicial system was decentralised and brought within their range for effective exercise of power.

To whom is the Judiciary finally accountable? A fair reply would again be: to the People of India. That immediately brings in the Legislature as assemblies of elected representatives of the people. But by Convention the legislatures are rightly barred from discussing the conduct of the judges. But why are the working of the judicial system or the procedure for the administration of justice never discussed in the legislatures?

Of course, the ultimate power of impeachment is vested in the Union Legislature but the procedure is so cumbersome, complicated and time-consuming that its efficacy as the instrument of control and accountability has been universally found to be non-existent. What is worse there is no graduated or structured mechanism of control. In the rarest of the rare circumstances when impeachment is resorted to it has failed to deliver the goods because the process tends to become politicised. In effect, it implies that for all practical purposes, in a de facto sense, in the High Court or the Supreme Court, a judge is not accountable, unless he breaks all the rules in the books!

To restore the judiciary on that high pedestal the entire judicial structure from the Gram Sarpanch and the Munsif to the Chief Justice of the Supreme Court needs to be redesigned and rebuilt on the foundations of merit and integrity. At every level, the black-sheep have to be spotted out ruthlessly and internal mechanism has to be devised for this purpose.

My first suggestion is that the judicial system in order to be truly independent has to be freed from the apron strings of the Executive. The legislatures both at the Central and in the States should allocate a fixed percentage of the revenue receipts for judicial administration which should be credited to a Judicial Fund of India to finance the autonomous working of a truly independent judicial system, from the Supreme Court down to the Munsif.

My second suggestion is that to ensure equality of access to the fountains of justice, the traditional one-to-one correspondence between the State/UT and a High Court should go. This would liberate the High Courts from pressures by the State Government. Indeed there may be more than one High Courts in the same State and no High Court in another, the latter being serviced by the High Court in the neighbouring State. The jurisdiction of the High Court should be worked out on the basis of the population of contiguous districts lying in one or more States/UT. There should not be a High Court with over 100 judges and another High Courts with just one or two. The High Courts should have more or less an equal number of judges. The sub-ordinate judiciary within the area of jurisdiction of a High Court should be under its control. The judges of the High Court should not be transferable to another High Court except at their own request or in fulfilment of the code of judicial conduct.

The Indian Judicial Service should be constituted. Law graduates should be recruited and trained (before they learn the tricks of the legal trade) by the National Judicial Service Commission, under the authority of the National Council of the Judiciary. Those who are inducted from the bar should be admitted to the cadre at the level of the District Judges or High Court Judges after going through a competitive examination of the LL.M. level.

The Chief Justice of the High Court should be selected out of the All India seniority list of High Court judges, on the basis of seniority-cum-fitness. The Supreme Court judges should be selected out of the Chief Justices of the High Courts. Both in the case of Chief Justice of India and the Chief Justices of the High Courts, the judges who do not have at least two or three years to retire should not be eligible. The senior judges who are thus bypassed should have the option to retire on the emoluments last drawn or be appointed as the Presiding Officers of Statutory Commissions or Tribunals. The judicial system does need a spring cleaning, a fresh look, once in a while. The Council, serving as the Controlling Authority of the cadre shall institute control mechanisms for regulating the conduct and behaviour of the member of the Judicial Service.

For in-house disciplinary measures, the laws of evidence should not be as strictly enforced as in ordinary prosecution. The verdict of the In-House Committee is bound to be respected by the judge indicted once he has lost the respect of his peers. Such an In-House Committee should function both in the High Court and the Supreme Court to probe allegations of nepotism, corruption, impropriety or misbehaviour.

It has been proposed that the Parliament (and the Assemblies) should have a Judicial Committee to decide allegations against sitting judge and report its findings to the Chief Justice. Dignity of the judiciary commands that, while they may be subject to evaluation of their peers, the members of the judiciary should not be exposed needlessly to public criticism or trial by the mass media. Because in many cases unfair criticism and baseless charges may be exploited.

The existing laws of contempt need to be watered down and any criticism of the working of the system or even a specific complaint against a judge in his judicial role should not be equated with contempt of the judiciary. A recent judgement of the Karnataka High Court has made an excellent recommendation in this regard.

Procedural reforms and transparency should plug many loopholes. Pending cases should be listed transparently and any deviation from the serial order should be clarified to the petitioners/plaintiffs involved in cases passed over. The progress of the cases should be published. The Supreme Court and the High Court may issue Daily Bulletins as in the case of the Parliament, on the progress of the cases.

The judges should not accept any favours from the Government or any gifts, directly or indirectly, from any private individual during their terms of office. They should not be re-employed in any capacity for five years after retirement. They may however accept honorary positions in the social field. At least while in service the judges should not nurse any expectation to be appointed to tribunals or commissions of inquiry or any office of profit after demission of office.

Just as the judge is liable, as a person, under the criminal or civil law, he should be liable under any law or rules pertaining to corrupt practices.

The real answer is decentralisation of the administration of justice and the revival of the Nyaya Panchayats. The Sarpanch and the Panches should be elected directly by the people for a short term from within the Panchayat. The next level should be Munsifs, who should be law graduates to administer justice at the Prakhand level. The Munsifs should be elected for a fixed term by the Prakhand Samitis. Similarly the Zila Parishad should elect the Zila Nyayadhish and his colleagues from out of the members of the Indian Judicial Service made available by the High Court or the Munsifs. The Zila Nyayadhish has to assisted by an appropriate number of Sahayak Nyayadhish, who should either be junior members of the IJS or the Munsifs from the Prakhands. At the High Court level, half the posts of judges should be filled by the District Judges on promotion and half by the members of the bar recommended on the basis of results of a test conducted by the NJSC and approved by the State Judicial Council, consisting of the Chief Justice of the High Court, the Chief Minister of the State, the Speaker of the Assembly, the Leader of the Opposition and the Chairman of the State Bar Council.

An interesting suggestion has been made recently by Shri N.M. Ghatate, Senior Advocate, to delink the Supreme Court from the State laws so that the High Courts concerned are the final authority in their case. That would have many advantages. The Supreme Court's authority would then be limited to the central laws which have a nation-wide application.

To sum up, it is not possible to eliminate the virus of corruption from the judicial system without substantial restructuring and procedural reform which will decentralise the administration of justice and bring it within reach of all at reasonable cost. Till then nothing but judicial conscience and censure by the peers can keep the virus under curb.

9

CHALLENGES TO THE JUDICIAL SYSTEM

R.K. Jain

Appointment/Transfer of Judges

It is time when a fresh look is needed in the process of appointment and transfer of judges. In the year 1993, a Bench of nine judges of the Supreme Court decided that Government will be bound to accept the recommendation of the Court in the matter of appointment of judges and three senior most judges of the Supreme Court will decide about the suitability or otherwise of a judge who is to be brought to the Supreme Court or the High Courts. This judgement is palpably wrong and needs reconsideration by a Larger Bench. The Parliament must come out with proper law for annulling this decision and restoring either the pre-1993 situation or making other suitable mechanism in which people have faith. In no country governed by the Rule of Law all over the world, the judges have the power to appoint judges. In no democracy elected representatives of the people have been kept out from the process of selecting the judges. What should be the shape of the judiciary, what type of judges the judicial system needs is basically the job of the elected representatives of the people. The present procedure obtaining after the 1993 judgement in the case of *S C Advocates-on-record Assn. vs. Union of India* in the appointment of judges, in all humility and respect for the judiciary is an affront to the democracy and the Constitution. The voice of Executive and elected representatives of the people must find its say in the appointment of judges because it is through them that the "Will" of the people is manifested. It is for the people of this country and not the judges alone to decide as to what type of judiciary the country needs. It is, therefore, of paramount importance that the procedure existing before 1993 for appointment of judges be restored by suitable legislation. It will also not be out of place to suggest that the Bar like in the USA should also be consulted before judges are appointed to the bench. To ignore this vital input will amount to undermining the importance of the Bar. The reason for incorporating the input from the bar for appointment of judges is simple. It is the members of the bar who see the judges in action day in and day out while arguing cases before them. It is also for this reason that the bar is the best judge of the judges. It is unfortunate that of late some self-appointed intellectuals have taken upon themselves the task of judging the judges. As a matter of fact the bar as a whole is the judge of the judges and not a miniscule minority claiming to be the guardian of all virtues. It further undermines the authority of judiciary when certain self-appointed conscious keepers of the judiciary recklessly issue statements not only with regard to the conduct of judges but also with regard to the decided cases without knowing the pleadings between the parties and the law on the subject. This trend is not very healthy and sooner an end is put to it, better it will be for the nation. It is the duty of each one of us to see that people of this great country continue to have faith in the judicial system until we find a better method of dispensation of justice. At a time when the stock of the Legislature and Executive is at all time low, any dent in the judicial system may ultimately result in breaking the country as happened in the Soviet Union. There is a lurking fear in the minds of people that there is concerted effort by certain vested interest to sabotage this institution. While it is possible that some people might be entertaining genuine apprehensions about the functioning of the judiciary, others it appears are acting at the behest of their outside masters inimical to the interest of this country. We have to guard ourselves against these elements. The authorities responsible for maintaining the sovereignty and integrity of India must act now and fast to unmask these forces. Fortunately these forces have not been able to cause much damage to the system, but if they get strength and encouragement from those in power they have the potential of misguiding the people of this country.

The Preamble of our Constitution reads thus:

"We, The People of India, having solemnly resolved to constitute India into a Sovereign Socialist Secular Democratic Republic and to secure to all its citizens:

Justice, social, economic and political;

Liberty of thought, expression, belief, faith and worship;

Equality of status and of opportunity;

and to promote among them all

Fraternity assuring the dignity of the individual and the unity and integrity of the Nation;

In our Constituent Assembly this twenty-sixth day of November, 1949, do Hereby Adopt, Enact and Give to Ourselves this Constitution."

Initially, instead of sovereign socialist secular democratic republic the words were sovereign democratic republic. By adding the word socialist secular, a heavy duty is cast on those deciding the matters relating to the Constitution that only those with socialist and secular credentials adorn the Bench of High Courts and Supreme Court. It will be the duty of the elected representative to see that only those who have ideology and social philosophy enshrined in the Preamble of the Constitution are elevated to the Bench. In such a situation, the judiciary as well as the elected representatives and the Executive must put their heads together to find suitable persons for these positions. The antecedents of the person concerned and his social leanings before he is appointed are very important and judges alone would be least competent to fulfil that job without proper inputs from the elected representative and the Executive.

Notwithstanding the above procedure for appointment of judges to the High Courts and Supreme Court, the system needs a radical change. High Courts and Supreme Court must have a composition which represents the geographical and sectional interest of all sections of the society. Every section of the society must feel that this court belongs to them also. Till about 2 years back there was not a single judge from Gujjar community throughout the country. Even now there are not very many Harijan judges in the High Courts. In the Supreme Court in the last fifty years we had only three judges belonging to the scheduled caste and scheduled tribes. This is not a very happy state. Similarly, the representation of the judges belonging to minority community is not adequate. I am not pleading for reservation of the scheduled caste and scheduled tribe and the minority on the Bench but the real question is that these sections must feel that their interest is safe in the hands of the Court and this will be possible only when they have proper representation on the Bench both in the High Courts and the Supreme Court subject to their passing the test of merit. A conscious effort will have to be made by those who are responsible for appointments to select suitable persons for High Courts and Supreme Court by giving proper representation to all sections of the society.

Independence of Judiciary

It needs no emphasis that the first and the foremost requirement of parliamentary form of Government is that judiciary should maintain complete independence from the influence of the Executive or the Legislature. However, care should be taken that the independence of judiciary is not to be raised to the level of a dogma so as to enable it to function as a kind of Super-Legislature or Super-Executive as opined by some of the members of the Drafting Committee of the Constitution.

At present judiciary is dependent on the Executive in financial matters. Even for providing increment to staff and small financial matters the Court has to look to the executive for release of funds. The dependence on the executive in financial matters interferes with the Independence of Judiciary. Dr. Ambedkar said once, "How can the judiciary be independent if they are financially dependent on the executives?" Therefore, it is imperative that Supreme Court and the High Courts should have complete financial autonomy. Their word should be last in the financial matters relating to the administration of justice. A section of the judiciary feels that the judges should not get involved in taking upon themselves matters relating to finance, but I feel that would be a short sighted view and would not be in the larger interest of the judiciary. Even the audit of the accounts of the judiciary should not be done by authorities outside the judiciary. Instances have come to light where the administration has put objections which were absolutely unwarranted. A committee headed by the Chief Justice of India, senior judges of the Supreme Court and senior Chief Justice of the High Courts should be formed to oversee all financial matters. The judiciary which has been given the task of deciding the fate of the nation in important matters, certainly can be entrusted with matters relating to its own finances. The sooner it is done, the better it is for the system.

It is sometimes forgotten that judiciary is one of the three organs of the State and has a place of pride in every democracy. A healthy judiciary is necessary for a healthy democracy. It is the duty of all concerned that the financial needs of the judicial system are reviewed annually. Each and every aspect of the expenditure of the judicial system, i.e., the judiciary and the Bar should be taken care of in the budget. Unless it is done no justice can be done to the system which is supposed to deliver justice to the entire society.

Successive Finance Ministers right from the independence have not thought it fit to place before the Parliament the financial needs of the judicial system in the Budget. It is high time that the Parliament looks into the matter and provides enough funds in the Budget so that even the weakest in the society gets complete justice in accordance with the mandate of the Constitution.

It is very unfortunate that till recently, no funds were earmarked for the judicial system. It was unplanned expenditure. I believe that of late a few hundred crores of rupees have been earmarked for the judicial system. This ad hoc allocation of a few hundred crores of rupees in the five-year plan does not serve any purpose. Like other items, every year there should be provision in the Budget for the judicial system after taking into consideration its needs.

India can justly be proud of her active, strong and independent judiciary. Our Hon'ble Judges and members of the Bar have lived up to the aspirations of the people and have strengthened our democratic polity. Although the system has weathered the onslaught from some scholars, politicians and other vested interests over almost five decades, it is time that we take a fresh look at the Constitution and various laws. After about forty-nine years of the working of the Constitution, it is high time that we take a fresh look at all the laws. The laws which have either become redundant with the passage of time or constitutionally unworkable must be removed from the statute book. The law must be as simple as possible so that the common man for whom the laws are made, is able to understand them without external aid. As far as possible, uniformity of laws throughout the country will be a welcome idea. The laws which are specially meant for the weaker sections of the society and those which are for general application, must, by some process, be well publicised so that people become aware of their rights and duties. For example, laws relating to landlords and tenants, house tax, water tax, property tax, electricity dues and consumer protection laws must be as simple as possible and must be available in all the languages. The salient features of the laws must be discussed on Television and Radio. The print media, particularly, the vernacular press must also help in this direction. The land reforms laws, land tenancy laws, zamindari abolition laws and law relating to consolidation of holdings, etc., should be made as simple as possible, so that the farmers know about their rights and unscrupulous elements in the society, in whatever field, are not able to exploit them. They should be made aware of the basic safeguards.

Judicial Activism

'Judicial Activism' cannot be defined in few words or in sentences because 'Judicial Activism' is understood by persons differently. To some it means positive and assertive role by the judiciary in enforcing the Constitutional Rights, more particularly the Fundamental Rights guaranteed to the citizens; to others it means disciplining and, if need be, dressing down the Executive and the Parliament; to some others it signifies performance by judiciary of some functions which do not strictly fall in the domain and jurisdiction of the judiciary and which ought to have been performed by the other wings of the State. For some it is an innovative measure initiated by the Supreme Court towards attaining Constitutionally ordained objectives in the form of Public Interest Litigation. To some others still, it may mean doing justice to the helpless silent majority who cannot approach the Court. However, one thing is definite that this Judicially Developed Weapon has done yeoman service to the suffering of millions and gone a long way in safeguarding individual liberty and fulfilling the social philosophy and other aims and objectives enshrined in our great Constitution.

The Constitution recognizes and embodies the doctrine of separation of powers of the three organs of the State namely the Executive, the Legislature and the Judiciary. Thus, broadly speaking the function of the Parliament is principally to enact laws; and of the Executive is to execute and comply with the laws so enacted. The function of the judiciary is to oversee and ensure that the Constitution and the laws of the land are obeyed by all howsoever high one may be and the other two organs of the State remain in their respective fields.

Thus, the power of judicial review (which is the basic feature of the Constitution) given by the Constitution to the judiciary makes the task of judiciary of paramount importance.

With the passage of time the judiciary realised that many cases of the infraction and infringement of the Constitutional rights go unredressed and unremedied because the affected persons are not able to knock the doors of justice due to their limitations such as poverty, illiteracy, social backwardness, lack of information and other resources. The court, therefore, vastly modified the principle of locus standi, so that the under-privileged, the downtrodden, the silent and the meek can air their grievances. This was the first but perhaps the most crucial step by the judiciary in taking justice to the doorstep of the poor.

The Indian judiciary took big strides when it consciously broadened the Fundamental Right to Life holding it to be the most Fundamental of the Fundamental Rights and read into it various facets of life holding that right to shelter, right to basic educationp, right to pollution free air and water, etc., fall within the expression 'life'.

Furthermore, it is only on the initiative and persistence of the Court that the Indian people and the industry have become so conscious of the serious threat to the ecological balance posed by the unplanned mushrooming of industry.

Of late the Indian judiciary has addressed itself to the deep-rooted problem of corruption in high offices. Thus, whether it is giving of national award or allotment of public houses or the allegation of corruption against the mighty politicians, the Hon'ble Supreme Court has clearly demonstrated that **'Be you howsoever high the law is always above you'**.

The Executive has generally not discharged its obligation to the society. The general perception of a common man is that vested interests and political, social and business circles control the Executives and so those who should be looked after by the society remain neglected. Without the interference of the judiciary the bonded labour could not have been freed. Even in the matter of abolition of Child Labour, Prison Reforms and undertrials, taking action against the erring industries in the matter of environment, the judiciary had to intervene. The illegal mining in Mussourie, Stone Crushers in Dehradun and erring Motor Vehicles in Delhi had to be disciplined by the judiciary.

Some critics of this activist approach of the judiciary needlessly fear that the judiciary is overstepping its limits by adopting the activist approach and that the judiciary is taking anti-majoritarian view in some cases. These critics, however, fail to realise that so long as the judiciary itself functions within the prescribed parameters of the Constitution, no exception can be taken merely because the effect and implication of their activist role cause discomfiture and displeasure to some who wield power. They also fail to see that more than the constitutional powers it is the unflinching faith and trust of the public in judiciary, which compels the judiciary to adopt an activist role in attending and asserting the plight of the silent masses. In fact, Judicial Activism is the need of the day.

There may be some aberrations here and there but they by themselves cannot condemn the entire system. It needs no emphasis that all the three organs of the state should remain their respective areas. There should be continuous interaction of all the three organs namely Judiciary, Legislature and Executive so that they can work together for larger public good. To insinuate motives when the leader of one organ meets the other would not only be wrong but prejudicial to the public interest. In fact, such interactions are very healthy for the public good. Frequent interactions among leaders are necessary so that they can understand better the problems faced by Indian People.

Alternative dispute redressal mechanism

Considering the mounting pressure of ever increasing litigation the courts are overburdened resulting in enormous delays in the disposal of the cases. It is the need of the hour that alternative and more efficacious dispute redressal mechanism is evolved to lighten the burden of the courts so that faster and less expensive justice is meted out to the litigants. Until we are able to find alternative forums, it is suggested that more and more Lok Adalats are held to tide over this problem.

10

INFLUENCE OF MEDIA ON JUDGES

P.P. Rao

The Constitution promises justice to one and all. It provides for a hierarchy of Courts and Tribunals for resolving disputes between the citizen and the State, between citizens themselves *inter-se,* and even disputes involving non-citizens. The right to judicial review is a basic feature of the Constitution. The Constitution recognises the doctrine of separation of powers and secures independence of Judiciary so that every judge and judicial officer may perform the duties of his office duly and faithfully and to the best of his or her ability, knowledge and judgement without fear or favour, affection or ill-will. In *L. Chandra Kumar vs. Union of India*[1], a Constitution Bench of seven judges declared that the power of judicial review is a basic and essential feature of the Constitution which cannot be taken away or abridged by any amendment of the Constitution.

In *K. Veeraswami vs. Union of India*[2], L.M. Sharma, J observed, "Judiciary has a duty to dispense justice between person and person as also between person and State itself". To be able to perform its duties effectively the Judges have to act "without fear or favour, affection or ill will." They must, therefore, be free from pressure from any quarter. Nobody can deny this basic essence of independence of judiciary. But for the judiciary to be really effective, the purity in the administration of justice and the confidence of the people in the courts are equally essential. It is to achieve this end that this higher judiciary has been vested with the power to punish for its own contempt. This has become necessary so that an aggrieved or misdirected person may not cast aspersions on the court which may adversely affect the public confidence. If the community loses its faith in the courts, their very existence will cease to have any meaning. A person with a just cause shall not approach the court for a legal remedy, if according to his belief the decision of the court would be given on extraneous consideration and not on the merits of his claim. People will return to the law of the jungle for settling their dispute on the streets.

Section 2(c.) of the Contempt of Courts Act, 1971 defines 'criminal contempt'. It includes the doing of any act which prejudices or interferes or tends to interfere with the due course of any judicial proceeding or obstructs or tends to obstruct the administration of justice in any manner. In District Magistrate, *Kheri vs. Hamid Ali*[3] the High Court of Oudh convicted the proprietor, printer and publisher of a newspaper of contempt of court for publishing an article which was clearly an attempt to prejudice the mind of the learned Magistrate in regard to the trial of the case pending in his court. Chief Justice Thomas in his judgement observed: "The newspapermen do not often realize at the time of writing that they are doing something improper or blameworthy. A journalist has no right to write in the tone the accused has used in the article on matters happening in law courts. The special privilege of the press is a time-worn fallacy, and the sooner the misconception that the press is not accountable to the law is removed the better it will be. No editor has a right to assume the role of investigator or try to prejudice the court against any person. Writing and publishing an article in a newspaper likely to prejudice the course of justice relating to pending case amounts to a contempt of court." In *Re: P.C. Sen*[4] the Supreme Court observed, "It is incumbent upon court of justice to preserve their proceedings from being misrepresented, for prejudicing the mind of the people against persons concerned as parties in causes before the case is finally heard has pernicious consequences....To make a speech tending to influence the result of a pending trial, whether civil or criminal is a grave contempt." The law in England is also the same. In *Attorney General vs. Times Newspapers Limited*[5] Lord Reid observed, "freedom of speech should not be limited to any greater extent than is necessary but it cannot be allowed where there would be real prejudice to the administration of justice." He further observed, "I think that there is a difference between direct interference with the fair trial of an action and words or conduct which may affect the minds of a litigant. Comment likely to affect the minds of witnesses and of the tribunal must be stopped for otherwise the trial may well be unfair."

Section 3 of the Contempt of Courts Act, 1971 clarifies that innocent publication and distribution of matter is not contempt of court. Section 4 says that a person shall not be guilty of contempt of court for publishing a fair and accurate report of a judicial proceeding or any stage thereof. As held by the Kerala High Court[6], "it is a well-settled proposition that reports of proceedings in Court in newspapers should be the faithful and fair reproduction thereof. There could also be no doubt that while reproducing the Court proceedings, no words might be added, omitted or substituted if their effect was to be more prejudicial to a party litigant than the actual proceedings; any deviation in the report from the correct proceedings actually recorded, if it offended the law of contempt of court, might render the alleged contemner liable to be proceeded against. Needless to say that the press reporter and the publisher of newspapers do not have any indefeasible right to put his own gloss on the statements in Court by selecting stray passages out of context which might have a tendency to convey to the reader to the prejudice of a party to the proceedings, a sense different from what would appear when the statement was read in its own context." V.R. Krishna Iyer J. observed in *Re: S. Mulgaokar*[7]: "the Fourth Estate which is an indispensable intermediary between the State and the people and necessary instrumentality in strengthening the forces of democracy, should be given free play within responsible limits even when the focus of its critical attention is the court, including the highest Court."

Apart from the power to punish for contempt, courts have power to prevent the publication of the evidence of witnesses during the course of the trial, if necessary. In *N.S. Mirajkar vs. State of Maharashtra*[8] a Constitution Bench of nine judges declared the law to this effect while upholding an order passed by V.M. Tarkunde J. in a case directing that the evidence of a particular witness should not be published. Ganjendragadkar J.

while recognising that public trial in open court is undoubtedly essential for healthy, objective and fair administration of justice, pointed out that this proposition is subject to exceptions. He said, "If the principle that all trials before courts must be held in public was treated as inflexible and universal and it is held that it admits of no exceptions whatever, cases may arise where by following the principle, justice itself may be defeated. That is why we feel no hesitation in holding that the High Court has inherent jurisdiction to hold a trial in *camera* if the ends of justice clearly and necessarily require the adoption of such a course." Last year the Supreme Court held in camera proceedings in Vineet Narayan's case. Section 17 of the 1971 Act deals with publication of information relating to proceedings in camera.

The media has a commitment to the basic human rights of accused persons in a country governed by rule of law. The manner in which certain sections of the media have covered politically important cases, particularly those monitored by the Supreme Court and High Courts, gives the impression that every politician accused of an offence deserves to be punished, trial or no trial, and should not be released on bail. As a result of indiscriminate media coverage of legal proceedings, public opinion started building up against the accused not only with respect to the charges which are yet to be tried, but also with respect to bail. Even after the discharge of most of the accused in the Jain Hawala case, the loss of reputation suffered by the accused leaders remains unsalvaged. It will remain an irreparable loss. Such opinion-building against the accused is not conducive to a fair trial consistent with basic human rights. The presumption of innocence itself is a basic human right—vide Art 11 of the Universal Declaration of Human Rights. The intention of the media is not to interfere with the course of justice or bring to bear public opinion assiduously built up by the media to affect decision-making in courts. The unintended effect of one-sided coverage without highlighting the basic human rights of accused persons is likely to interfere with the course of justice and result in miscarriage of justice. Strictly speaking, it is contempt of court to build up public opinion against accused persons in any criminal case. In the words of Lord Reid[9].

"anything in the nature of prejudgement of a case or of specific issues in it is objectionable not only because of its possible effect on that particular case but also because of its side effects which may be far-reaching. Responsible 'mass-media' will do their best to be fair, but there will also be ill-informed, slapdash or prejudiced attempts to influence the public. If people are led to think that it is easy to find the truth disrespect for the processes of the law could follow and, if mass media are allowed to judge, unpopular people and unpopular causes will fare very badly. Most cases of prejudging of issues fall within the existing authorities on contempt."

Media coverage of court proceedings is necessary. At the same time, it is the duty of the media to emphasise the pre-requisites of a fair trial and the basic human rights of accused persons including the right to bail pending investigation and trial. Media coverage should not be allowed unwittingly to become media intrusion in administration of justice. The criminal justice system remains the same irrespective of the nature of offence and the position of an accused. Such a system which assures a fair trial even to a person accused of the heinous offence of murder cannot deny the human rights to political leaders accused of economic offences. It is the duty of every institution and individual to uphold the human rights and facilitate their enforcement in any civilised society.

Justice R.S. Sarkaria in a speech[10] delivered by him as the then Chairman, Press Council of India on World Freedom Day on May 3, 1994 at U.N. Information Centre, New Delhi, stated as follows: "It will not be out of place to mention here that it was disclosed at the International Conference held in Stockholm in June, 1991, that when the Swedish Prime Minister (Mr. Olfe Palme) was assassinated and the suspect was arrested and put on trial, the Swedish Press did not disclose the identity of the assailant before he was tried and convicted by the trial court. This is, one of the salutary norms of journalistic ethics which is being observed meticulously in Sweden though there is no law as such of contempt of court in that country."

"It is the function and right of the media to gather and convey information to the public and to comment on the administration of justice including cases before, during and after trial, without violating the presumption of innocence."

"The basic principle does not exclude the preservation by law of secrecy during the investigation of crime even where investigation forms part of the judicial process. Secrecy in such circumstances must be regarded as being mainly for the benefit of persons who are suspected or accused, to preserve the presumption of innocence."

Freedom of speech and expression itself is a basic human right, but not an absolute right. It is subject to reasonable restrictions. One such restriction is that it shall not be exercised in a manner so as to influence the mind of the judge in a pending case or so as to cause prejudice to the accused person. The right to a fair trial is basic to the rule of law. It is the duty of the media to respect this right and also appreciate that it is the duty of a judge to arrive at a correct decision in every case objectively uninfluenced by extraneous considerations. If media publicity becomes a factor reckon with for a judge or a court that will be the beginning of the end of the rule of law. The role of media in the O.J. Simpson trial is not an example worthy of emulation. Judges are human beings. After the advent of electronic media, the tendency to render populistic judgements or pass orders which would hit the headlines is, regrettably, on the increase. This is a disturbing trend. In this context the suggestion made by Justice P.B. Sawant, Chairman, Press Council that while reporting court news it would be better not to mention the names of judges in the media deserves serious consideration.

REFERENCES

1. (1997) 3 SCC 261
2. (1991) 3 SCR 189, 264
3. AIR 1940 Oudh 137
4. AIR 1970 SC 1821, 1824, 1825
5. 1973 3 All ER 54
6. 1984 C ri.L.J. 1061
7. (1978) 3 SCR 162, 175
8. (1966) 3 SCR 744, 755
9. A.G. vs. Times Newspaper Ltd. (1973) 3 All ER 54, 65
10. The Press Council of India Review (1994) Vol. 15 pp. 1 at 7

11

ACCOUNTABILITY OF JUDGES

Hardev Singh

How to Judge the Judges?

Who is competent and what is the criterion?

These are questions that arise at the threshold. Judging really means the authority to subject a judge to adjudicatory process, pronounce verdict and administer appropriate punishment.

There is, however, a broader area of judging which belongs to the field of public opinion. This is no less important because the judges in discharge of their duties of the public office sit on judgement over others.

The locus to judge cannot be circumscribed in a democratic set up. The consumer of justice—those who are affected, have the locus. Additionally press, academicians, commentators, members of the public and their representatives have the locus.

It is not possible to think of a judge who sits on judgement over fellow beings unless the person has unblemished character and judicial rectitude. Honesty uprightness, integrity and basic learning are essential qualities of a judge.

Then there is the philosophy that determines the approach a judge adopts in administering justice. The philosophy emanates from the Constitution that we gave unto ourselves on January 26,1950. Though the Constitution is written, it is interpreted and practised differently and sometimes at complete variance with its letter and spirit.

One does not have to embark upon an exhaustive discourse to discover the philosophy embodied in the Constitution. The historical background leading to the framing of the Constitution is indispensable for understanding it. The Constitution for independent India after long-drawn arduous struggle was framed to constitute a Sovereign Socialist Secular Republic that would secure to the multitude of the exploited millions Justice, Liberty, Equality and Fraternity.

The running thread of the philosophy of the Constitution is epitomised in the preamble and elucidated in Part-II, and Part-III, the later of which is meant to be put into practice by the State progressively.

The mandate of the Constitution is all the more meaningful because a judge upon entering into office takes oath to uphold the Constitution.

The Constitution envisaged change from the colonial rule to governance of the people, representing diversities based upon caste, creed, religion, culture who borne freedom after prolonged struggle. It is equally true that a new judicial system was envisaged to realise these aspirations. The judicial system means the body of laws, substantive and procedural. The judge steers the judicial machinery and administers justice.

The process of judging a judge comprises not only judging his character and behaviour but his philosophy as well. This in a way goes to judging the system and how far the philosophy of a judge is in consonance with it.

It has to be borne in mind that the higher judiciary is not accountable in our constitutional scheme. A widespread demand has been in the offing to make the judiciary accountable and render its functioning transparent. The Committee on Judicial Accountability comprising representatives of the Bar came into being at an All India Convention held in 1991. All these and allied questions engaged the Committee and after careful and prolonged deliberations, the Committee finalised draft of a Bill to provide for constitution of a National Judicial Commission to whom would be entrusted the matters of appointment, removal and transfer of judges.

The proposal to constitute National Judicial Commission was finalised after past experience, particularly the Ramaswami episode which exposed the utter futility of machinery provided by Article 124 of the Constitution. The Committee on Judicial Accountability arrived at the conclusion that short of constitutional amendment the higher judiciary will remain totally unaccountable.

The proposed bill provides for insertion of Chapter III-A with insertion of a new Article 123-A providing for constitution of the National Judicial Commission to deal with the appointment, transfer and removal of judges of the Supreme Court and High Courts. The Commission is designed to be a high body independent of the Executive and the Judiciary. Articles 124, 126, 217 and 222 are substituted by new Articles suitably amended to fall in line with the scheme envisaged by Article 123-A.

What has to be seen is that the Constitutional mechanism provided for judging the judges in a narrow sphere of what is called 'misbehaviour' by a judge. The trial that a judge may be put to is akin to the criminal trial where charges require to be proved to the hilt.

So what we see is that there are two aspects of the process of judging the judges. Judging by the judicial machinery clothed with sentencing power is within a very narrow compass. A judge in this case can only be judged for a culpable offence under criminal law or infraction of some rule having the force of law.

The question of judging a judge in respect of broader ambit adverted to above is outside the purview of constitutional machinery. But yet judging the judges on matters outside the purview of criminal culpability are vital to the system of justice. This aspect falls within the arena of "Public Justice" if one may use the expression.

The building of public opinion regarding the behaviour, philosophy and conduct of a judge is an effective and valuable right in the hands of those who are not vested with the power and authority to punish a judge for misbehaviour under the Constitution. This right must be exercised whenever occasion arises because of the near futility and inefficacy of the constitutional machinery.

The legal fraternity who are an essential part of judicial machinery have special duty to oversee the performance of a judge and assist in formation of public opinion. Members of the Bar are not only suited but better placed for this role because of their being part of the system and being connected with its functioning.

Yet there is interlinking of the two modes of judging the judges, i.e., by resort to the constitutional machinery and the formation of public opinion. This interlinking is demonstrated by an instance when Bombay Bar passed a resolution deprecating the conduct of Chief Justice Bhattacharjee pursuant to which he demitted office. The basis upon which the Bar formed its opinion touched upon misbehaviour on part of the judge. It is a different matter that the Supreme Court in a public interest litigation frowned upon taking resort to this course by the Bar. In the case of *Ravichandran Iyer (JT 1995(5) SC 339)* Chief Justice Bhattacharjee of Bombay High Court demitted office after he was subjected to criticism touching upon his conduct and behaviour. The Supreme Court (Justice K. Ramaswami) observed that "in case the allegations are against Chief Justice of a High Court, the Bar should bring them directly to the notice of the Chief Justice of India." Further, the observations that the Bar Association or a group of advocates "are prohibited to discuss the conduct of a judge in the discharge of his duties or pass any resolution in that behalf."

This decision and observations made by the learned judge rather than settle the crucial question poses matters of great moment for debate. Besides the fundamental right of speech and expression matters touching upon independence of judiciary, accountability of higher judiciary, transparency of its functioning and purity of the system of justice are some of the questions that cry for public debate.

What has been said above shows that the matter of judging the judges requires a more in-depth study and public debate. It certainly does not admit of simplistic treatment.

12

INDEPENDENCE OF JUDICIARY AND JUDGING THE JUDGES

Abhishek Singhvi

Whenever subjects as significant as Independence of Judiciary and Judicial Accountability are discussed, it is vital to recognise that these are not mere cliche but are imbued with practical form and content. The proposition of independence of judiciary is so axiomatic as to be almost superfluous: no independent judiciary, no rule of law. Independence of Judiciary, therefore, occupies slots of pristine glory everywhere—it is there in the United Nations Universal Declaration in the International Covenant, the European Convention, the American Convention and in a diverse array of international law generating documents. Most significantly, it is the subject of specific United Nations sponsored studies on the Independence of Justice[1] leading to vital declarations on the independence of justice at Montreal and the formulation of draft principles on independence of justice.

And yet, in a strange inversion of Rousseau's warning—"Man is free, but is everywhere in chains," one finds independence of justice axiomatic everywhere in principle and yet its violation pathologically pervasive. The immutable words of the inimitable Krishna Iyer sum up the malady:

> Indeed, the very Court System is under furious pressure in many countries and its functional independence is sought to be subverted by stratagems, scuttled by covert or overt tactics and enticed by occupational bonuses. Genetic engineering, in the sense of hand-picking personal favourites or Party nominees, screening and

manipulating candidates even at the time of recruitment so as to ensure judicial genuflexion or secret loyalty and eliminating persons of probity and wisdom and social conscience is one method of undermining independence. Similarly, during the career of Judges, many carrots are held out to deflect judicial performance from the path of rectitude. Judicial afternoons and evenings are sensitive phases, the incumbent being bothered about post-retiral prospects. The Executive plays upon this weakness to bend the integrity or buy the partiality of the elderly brethren. Survival after tenurial death is a spell the Executive, with its vast reservoir of patronage, uses to purpose and the robed brethren, save the robust, succumb. Moreover, the judiciary as an institution, is itself subjected to attack or is hijacked, criticised, misrepresented, debunked, budgetarily humbled and in many innovative ways made to feel that it is in their interests to toe the line. Constitutional guarantees are muscled or menaced by parliamentary plurality and executive authority. Having neither the purse nor the sword, the Judiciary yields.[2]

I have no doubt that this malady will continue, nay deepen and is likely to assume epidemic proportions unless we pay immediate and sustained attention to the two crucial aspects of judicial appointments and judicial accountability.

Turning to the first, it is a telling reflection of the times that our systems of judicial appointments are so subjective and shrouded in secrecy that possibly none of the elements of a "great" judge are subjected to the dialectics of the selection and appointment process. A.U.S. survey of great judges issued questionnaires to fellow court watchers. Sixty-five academic observers were asked to grade the judges in 1970: 12 greats, 15 near-greats, 55 average, 6 below average and 8 failures emerged. Chief Justice Marshall got all 65 votes as great, Brandeis 62, Holmes 61 and Black 42. The other 8 greats, in chronological order, were Sotry, Taney, Harlan, Hughes, Stone, Cardozo, Frankfurter and Warren.

The organiser of the survey deduced that greatness resulted from a combination of the following qualities:

1. Scholarship
2. Legal learning and analytical powers
3. Craftsmanship and technique
4. Wide general knowledge and learning
5. Character, moral integrity and impartiality
6. Diligence and industry
7. The ability to express oneself orally with clarity, logic and compelling force
8. Openness to change
9. Courage to take unpopular decisions
10. Dedication to the court as an institution and to the office of Supreme Court Justice
11. Ability to carry a proportionate share of the court's responsibility in opinion-writing, and finally
12. The quality of statesmanship.[3]

We must ask ourselves if the appointments process ever makes even an attempt to identify or apply these criteria.

In a sense, the appointments process as far as India is concerned has been a collective one. But the debate is not regarding its collective nature but regarding how broad based that collectivity should be and secondly, how open its selection process should be. India since independence till 1993 experienced executive primacy in judicial appointments but tempered by consultation between the executive and the judiciary. This executive primacy theory was upheld in *S.P. Gupta's decision* in 1982. It has been substituted since 1993 by judicial primacy—including, in cases of lack of consensus by Chief Justice primacy—coupled with what the 1993 Supreme Court judgement calls "integrated participatory consultative process" amongst the three seniormost judges.

Unfortunately, the sad truth is that neither of these two "primal" or "primus" theories appears to have worked well, although in all fairness, it must be conceded, that the current system has been in operation only since 1993. A lot can be said about the dangers inherent in substituting absolute executive authority with absolute Chief Justice authority. If absolute and sole authority is unwise, would Lord Action's warning against power and absolute power apply any the less to the judiciary? The time may well now have come for a more broad based appointing body, incorporating undoubtedly the highest judicial functionaries but also giving representation to some outside elements from the categories of eminent jurists, academics and both the ruling executive and the opposition. Moreover, this process would certainly be more transparent and open. Each country ultimately has to find its own golden Aristotelian mean and that I believe has to be between the two extremes of the British absolute unfettered executive discretion shrouded in secrecy, choosing from a minute homogeneous club spreading over 1 square mile in London and the equally unacceptable American model relying upon the stripping naked of a potential appointee under the harsh glare of media lights with sensationalism taking the place of substance, trivia doing service for totality and salacious scandal substituting for sound decision making.

The second crucial aspect needing urgent attention is the vital necessity of a workable mechanism for regulating judicial conduct, taking corrective action and, if necessary, disciplining errant judges short of and up to removal. To adopt the words of Jerome Frank, while the judicial robe can conceal the physical contours of the man, it cannot be allowed to continue to be an all encompassing shroud of secrecy. Laski's advice must be heeded:

> Obviously, therefore, the men who are to make justice in the courts, the way in which they are to perform their function, the methods by which they are to be chosen, the terms upon which they shall hold power, these and their related problems, lie at the heart of political philosophy. When we know how a nation-State dispenses justice, we know with some exactness the moral character to which it can pretend.[4]

We all know that impeachment is available, but as Krishna Iyer has said, this is like a Penal Code providing only for one extreme punishment, viz., death sentence and nothing else. All countries are experiencing increasing attacks and assaults on individual judges and these barbs, arrows, potshots and cannons will only increase not decrease unless we put in place a reasonable, internal, fair, expeditious and effective inhouse regulatory regime short of impeachment. The present all or nothing approach will inexorably push allegations against judges first to salacious bar room gossip and then to uninformed street chat unless you provide both the genuinely aggrieved complainant and the motivated maverick with a single uniform avenue to channel his grievances.

A code of conduct, internally evolved and applied, is undoubtedly a core component of this internal regulatory regime but is by no means the end of it.

The system must have a redressal mechanism with well laid down procedures, albeit internal, and must culminate in a final result one way or the other within a time bound schedule. The action taken, be it admonition, warning, request, transfer or curtailment of jurisdiction or anything more drastic must be done discreetly, internally, quietly and soberly but must nevertheless exit in a real and meaningful manner.

Lastly, I must touch upon the fact that the dangers to the independence of the judiciary are no less from within than from without. Many countries, in this region including India, have many telling examples of such threats from within; including recent events of a distasteful nature. There is clearly no bottom line in such matters. But if you sow the wind you must be prepared to reap the whirlwind and that too uncomplainingly. If you do not take care while appointing judges, there is precious little you can do except complain when your appointee takes a pot shot at you. Equally, when you apply policies of appointment or transfer or work allocation in an arbitrary or whimsical manner, you create and expand what I consider to be the most dangerous species on earth, viz., the class of frustrated, angry judges, working under a cross which they want to throw back at the system as also at individuals who run the system. An unhappy or a frustrated judge is a time bomb waiting to explode and his implosion is far more destructive within than outside the system.

REFERENCES

1. Singhvi, L.M., Special Rapporteur, UN Study *on the Independence and Impartiality of the Judiciary, Judges and Assessors and the Independence of Lawyers* (31.7.85; E/CN 4/ Sub2/1985/18)
2. Iyer, Krishna, *Justice at Crossroads,* 1992, pp. 60-61.
3. Simon, Lee, *Judging Judges,* 1988, p. 124.
4. Laski, Harold J., *A grammar of Politics,* pp. 541-42.

13

CRIMINAL JUSTICE SYSTEM IN INDIA

K.T.S. Tulsi

To strike a balance between the needs of the law enforcement agencies on the one hand, and protection of the citizens from harassment at the hands of the same agencies, on the other, is a perennial problem of statecraft. In the 20th century, it seems that the pendulum has swung from one extreme, the one in favour of the enforcement agencies, to the other, reflecting concern for the citizens. Even in the beginning of the 20th century, Justice Holmes declared:

> At the present time in this century, there is more danger that criminals will escape justice than that they will be subjected to tyranny.

At the close of the 20th century, the words of Justice Holmes ring even more true. This is evident from the steep rise in crime on the one hand, and decline in convictions, on the other. The number of murders in India increased by 294 per cent between 1953 and 1994. The rise in the cases of rape is even more steep – 431 per cent. The situation with regard to the efficacy of the Criminal Justice System can be best judged not only from the percentage increase of the crimes (which can partly be attributed to increase in population), but from the corresponding decline in convictions. The conviction rate in India is perhaps one of the lowest in the world. It is so low that law has practically ceased to be a deterrent for the offenders. The low rate of convictions can also be responsible for the rapid rise in the rate of crime amongst the educated and the urban population. It is the rare possibility of convictions which demoralises the honest and emboldens the unscrupulous. The society cannot continue to look down upon persons accused of horrendous crimes, when at the end of the long-drawn trial, 94 out of 100 return, flaunting acquittals—the stigma of criminality removed and washed by the courts. It is this trend, which finds large number of persons accused of serious offences, returning to legislatures claiming to be the nation builders in the right earnest. It is the victims, the witnesses, the prosecutor and the judges who look sheepishly away while the offender proudly stalk the exhaulted chambers of legislatures.

According to the statistics available from the National Crime Records Bureau, a murder is committed somewhere in the country every 13 minutes, meaning thereby that on an average, 106 murders are committed in the course of every 24 hours somewhere or the other in the country. If the police succeeds in solving every murder case and if in all the 106 cases of murder that were committed in the course of the last 24 hours, one person was arrested in each case, going by the current rate of convictions, 100 of those arrested will be acquitted and only six will ultimately be convicted and undergo their sentence.

Consider the case of rape. A rape is committed somewhere in the country every 40 minutes. Thirty-seven women are raped in different parts of the country in the course of 24 hours. If the police were able to track down every rapist and assuming that only one person was involved in each rape, 37 rapists can be assumed to have been arrested. Arrest is an important step in the course of investigation, which is made on the basis of sufficient material available with the police, to raise a strong suspicion against a person regarding his involvement in a non-cognizable offence. An arrest, according to law, cannot be made as a matter of course. It is a serious invasion of a citizen's liberty which cannot be taken away without substantial cause. But, after all the 37 persons go through the rigour of trial in a Court of law, given the current statistics, 35 of the alleged rapists arrested by the police and put on trial will earn respectable acquittals with the aid of benefits of doubt. Two out of the 37 will, however, have to undergo imprisonment. Considering the rate of convictions, the gamblers amongst potential offenders are bound to find it to be an attractive proposition.

With the advances in the mode of communications and movements, while the detection of crime has become more difficult, conspiracies to defeat the law has become more organised. The most favoured legislative exercise to arrest increase in crime is making the law more stringent by way of providing for 'presumptions' and 'reversal of burden of proof'. Whether these were the offences against society in the field of food adulteration or corruption or Foreign Exchange Regulation or violations of customs and excise laws and more recently terrorist offences or smuggling of narcotics drugs. Neither the presumptions nor the reversal of burden of proof have proved to be an answer to the problem. Statistics show that more stringent the laws, lesser the convictions.

No Place for the Victim

The legislatures have, therefore, necessarily to give the problem of rising crime and dwindling convictions, a deep thought. Rough and ready solutions have failed to work, suggesting that these were perhaps not the problems in the first instance. The problem with our Criminal Justice System seems to be that it has become completely insensitive to the victim. While it is true that in many cases it is not even possible to identify the victim, like in the case of certain offences under the Prevention of Corruption Act, Prevention of Food Adulteration Act, Smuggling of narcotics and arms etc. but even in those cases where the victim is identifiable, there is no place for him in the Court. Look at the structure of a Courtroom. It has a fixed place for a judge, the accused, the prosecutor, the witness and an earmarked place for the public, but it has no place for the victim. The victim has no say in the proceedings. The state is supposed to represent the victim and where the victim is not identifiable, to represent the people in general. That may perhaps be the weakest link in the 20th century Criminal Court, not only in India, but also in the entire western world.

Prosecutors

Separation of investigation from prosecution may have been desirable from many points of view, but it seems to have contributed to the decline in the conviction rates. As a result of the separation, it was hoped that prosecution would become more independent and fair. That may be true but one of the ill-effects of the separation has also been that investigation seems to lose interest in the case as soon as the charge-sheet is filed. Thereupon, the case is considered to be the baby of the prosecution even while the prosecutor has no means to investigate the loose ends, left unprobed by the investigation. He has no means to secure the presence of the witnesses. He has no means of locating the witness who may have shifted base. Every case of acquittal is blamed by the prosecutor on poor investigation and by the investigation on ineffective prosecution. In the end, it is the cause of justice which suffers. We need to examine the American system, where not only does the institution of criminal cases rest with the prosecuting attorney, but he is authorised to intervene and exclusively control the investigation under the overall control of the Attorney General of the State. Such a modification in the Criminal Procedure Code would greatly harmonise the functioning of the investigating and the prosecuting agencies and could result in better coordination amongst the two.

Witness

The second weakest link in the Criminal Justice System is the witness. The Criminal Court can only rely on the witness as to acquaint itself of the truth and render justice. For the non-availability of the natural, honest and reliable witnesses, the Criminal Justice System has no one but itself to blame. Even if honest citizens were willing to assist the Criminal Justice System, the extent of harassment, witnesses are subjected to, by the system is so enormous that no one except the close relations and friends undertake the trouble of assisting the Criminal Justice System, as witnesses. This itself has reduced the credibility of the system. Investigating Officers need to realise that their entire labour will come to a nought if harassment of the citizens at the police stations, and at the scene of crime does not stop. The Investigating Officer needs to understand that he needs the witness much more and not vice versa. Witnesses cannot be made to wait from morning to evening either by the Investigating Officers or by the Courts, for lending assistance to the Criminal

Justice System. So long as the police stations and the Courtrooms fail to provide minimum courtesy and comfort to the witnesses, the Courts will continue to get less independent and less honest witnesses, resulting in decline in the quality of criminal justice.

We need to give a serious thought to an exhaustive *Witness Protection Programme,* if the courts want to be relevant in the nation's fight against militancy and terrorism. Mere provision for holding the trial in camera under TADA Act, proved to be woefully inadequate to convince the witness that they will be saved of retribution, at the hands of dangerous terrorists. I was myself a Special Prosecutor, assigned the task of prosecuting some of the cases against dreaded terrorists. Dilip Singh's son, Avtar Singh had been shot dead in his presence by M.S. Ajnala, Sukhdev Singh Gorengal, G.S. Tohra and Geja Singh at 1.00 pm on February 6, 1988. The accused came armed with AK-47 rifles, knocked at the doors of Dilip Singh's house and took him near the church of the village. M.S. Ajnala was alleged to have shot Avtar Singh in front of Dilip Singh. Ajnala was arrested after he surrendered at the Golden Temple during Operation Black Thunder. The confession was recorded by the Superintendent of Police on videotape. I met Dilip Singh shortly before his deposition in the Court. With tears in his eyes, he politely told me that he would not be able to speak in the Court or identify Ajnala, for if he did so, his two other sons would meet the same fate. I tried to assure him that we would not mention his name in the records. But Dilip Singh knew the reality better than I. The FIR was already on record and so were a host of other documents. Ajnala belonged to the same village. His identity could never be kept secret. Dilip Singh refused to identify Ajnala and the case ended in acquittal.

If the same trial had taken place in the United States, Dilip Singh would have been given a different name; would have been given a same kind of land in a different village in a different state; his name in the voters list would have been included; all his children would have been given similar jobs in the other states and Dilip Singh too, would have been given a similar job in a different state. Under those circumstances, Dilip Singh would have taken the side of justice.

We must seriously consider adopting the *Witness Protection Programme* without which the Courts will simply not be able to dispense true justice. I also remember the case in which Daya Singh, the brother of Nirmal Singh, Sarpanch, was killed in Beas on April 21, 1988, or the case of Swaran Kaur, whose husband Gurdial Singh was shot dead by five youths, who entered her house by breaking down the door, or the case of Rakesh Kumar whose father Bhagwan Das, and seven other relatives were shot dead allegedly by Amar Singh and Satnam Singh Satta. None of them were willing to depose for fear of retribution.

Lastly, the Courts must take into account, the hard realities of society—the hard realities of our social fabric. Absence of natural witnesses cannot invariably lead to adverse inferences. Reluctance of honest, unconcerned persons, is becoming more and more difficult to secure. If we continue to suspect the bonafides of police, it can only get further demoralised. If the accused continue to earn acquittals by default, the courts only place an enormous power in the hands of the police officials to screen the offenders. The victim cannot be made to pay for the lapses of investigation, because it is the victim or the society which eventually pays for unmerited acquittals. Insistence on 'proof beyond doubt', cannot be permitted to become insistence on removal of all doubts. Doubts must be of reasonable nature as understood by reasonable men, in the same situation in which the crime is committed and no doubts raised by fertile imagination of brilliant lawyers.

Maybe the time has come for us to consider the involvement of common men like jurors, with the Criminal Justice System. Sometimes ordinary men can provide better results than the independent, the educated and the articulate. The matter in any event, brooks no delay. We can wait no longer. In any case, what can we wait for? Are we to wait for the conviction rate to drop from the measly 6.4 per cent? The legislature needs to act and act fast, because the first responsibility of the state is to administer effective Criminal Justice System.

14

JUDICIAL ACTIVISM—HOW WISE, HOW OTHERWISE?

Surat Singh

Judicial Activism Defined

These days in India people are talking about intervention of judiciary in many spheres of activities which were traditionally assigned to other wings of the Government. For example, recently there were intervention of judiciary in allotment of petrol pumps by Petroleum Minister, allotment of housing by Minister of Housing, etc. Similarly, Supreme Court has intervened as to how the elections of political parties like Janata Dal are to be held. Even Supreme Court is considering the case whether the transfer of CBI Director Mr. Joginder Singh by Ministry of Home Affairs is valid or not.

So judicial activism means intervention of judiciary in the decisions of policy-making in areas traditionally assigned to other wings of government, like executive or legislative.

But the real question is whether such kind of intervention by judiciary in fields traditionally assigned to other wings of government is wise or otherwise. In this connection, it will be helpful to take a quick review of dominant trends of the Supreme Court decision making over last five decades. If we review the last fifty years of Indian Supreme Court since its inception in 1950, the following dominant trends will emerge:

(i) Period of excessive deference towards legislative and executive wings of the Government (1950 to 1966)

To cite one example, in *A.K. Gopalan vs. State of Madras 1950,* the Indian Supreme Court took a very conservative view of its own powers. In that case A.K. Gopalan, a Communist was preventively detained by the government. He challenged the validity of his detention on the ground that he had been deprived of his liberty in an unlawful manner. It was argued on his behalf that Article 21 of the Constitution should be liberally interpreted like the due process clause in the 14th Amendment of American Constitution. In other words, like American interpretation of due process, in India also, nobody should be deprived of his liberty without providing reasonable opportunity of hearing to him before taking any adverse action against him. The exact language of Article 21 of the Constitution of India is that no person shall be deprived of his life or personal liberty except according to a procedure established by law.

So, it was argued that the term 'Procedure established by law' under Article 21 of the Constitution should be interpreted as only proper, reasonable and fair procedure as it is the position in the USA.

But the first Chief Justice of India Mr. Justice Harilal J. Kania rejected this argument and gave a narrow interpretation to the term procedure established by law. The Supreme Court by a majority vote held that procedure established by law means any procedure which has been laid down by a competent legislature whether proper or improper. The Supreme Court will not enquire into the reasonableness or the wisdom of the procedure. Such was the excessive deference for the legislative wing of the government in 1950s.

(ii) Zealous protector of fundamental rights. *For example, in Golak Nath vs. State of Punjab (1966)*

The Supreme Court under the leadership of Chief Justice Mr. K. Subba Rao held that even the Parliament does not have any power to abridge or take away any of the fundamental rights from the date of the decision in that case. In that case the land ceiling laws and land reforms amendments were challenged on the ground that they took away the fundamental right of property of the landowners in violation of Article 31 of the Constitution. On behalf of the government it was argued that Parliament has the power to amend any part of the Constitution including Part-III of the Constitution which included Fundamental Rights. But the Supreme Court rejected this argument and held that even Parliament under its amending powers cannot take away or abridge the Fundamental Rights of the people. When the question arose as to what will happen to the laws already passed in violation of Fundamental Rights since 1950, the Supreme Court suggested the solution of prospective over-ruling, meaning thereby that the decision of the Supreme Court will apply from the date of decision in future only and in future Parliament will have no power to amend or take away the Fundamental Rights to the disadvantage of the citizen. Such was the attitude of the Supreme Court towards other wings of the government after departure of leaders like Nehru from the political scene.

(iii) Self-declared protector of Fundamental Values of the Constitution

In the most important case of Indian Supreme Court namely *Keshava Nand Bharti vs. State of Kerala (1973)* all the 13 judges of the Supreme Court sat for 69 days to hear the top legal luminaries to consider the question whether Parliament can amend any part of the Constitution including Fundamental Rights? Whether Golak Nath was rightly decided? What is the scope of amending powers of the Parliament?

It is interesting to note that the Supreme Court was equally divided (6 : 6) whether Indian Supreme Court should follow the British model of Parliamentary Supremacy or it should follow the American system of dominance of written constitution interpreted by the Supreme Court. The 6 judges took the view that India has adopted the West Minister model of Parliamentary democracy and the final word should be left with the elected representative of the people and they should feel free to change or amend any part of the Constitution according to their understanding of the situation and they took the view that there should not be any limitation on the amending power of the Parliament. On the other hand, the 6 other judges took the view that if legislature can change any part of the Constitution, then what was the point in having a written Constitution and how the fundamental rights of the people will be protected against legislative intrusion.

It is remarkable that the 13th judge Hon'ble Mr. Justice H.R. Khanna tilted the balance by throwing his vote with those six judges who favoured the limitation on the amending power of Parliament and who has advocated the American system. So it was decided that though Parliament has vast power of amending any part of the Constitution but it cannot take away or abridge the Basic Structure of the Constitution or Basic Features of the Constitution. However, there was no unanimity of opinion about the exact contents of the so called Basic Structure of the Constitution except that democratic form of the government could not be converted into dictatorship or Republican Form of Government or into hereditary form of the Government.

So Indian Supreme Court in the above-mentioned landmark judgement intervened more deeply and pervasively than even the American Supreme Court ever imagined to. So it was the most glaring example of judicial activism in Indian contexts.

(iv) The implementation of Basic Structure theory against Smt. Indira Gandhi herself (1976)

In *Smt. Indira Gandhi vs. Raj Narain (1976),* the occasion arose whether the elections of the Prime Minister could be placed beyond judicial review?

As it may be recalled that in June 1975, the then Prime Minister Mrs. Indira Gandhi's election as a Member of Parliament was held to be vitiated by corrupt practices as per Allahabad High Court and the appeal was pending before the Supreme Court. In the meantime, Mrs. Indira Gandhi declared emergency to save her chair and she sent opposition leaders behind the bars. She managed to pass an amendment to the Constitution which provided that the elections of the Prime Minister as well as the Speaker of the Lower House will not be open to be questioned in any court of law. The validity of this amendment came up for consideration in the above case and the Supreme Court struck down the impugned amendment as violative of the

Basic Structure of the Constitution. This is a glorious example of judicial activism to save Indian democracy. But this kind of judicial independence did not continue during the dark period of emergency from 1975 to 1977 as indicated below:

(v) The Dark Period of Emergency and the retreat of Judiciary in its cell

In *ADM Jabalpur vs. Shukla,* decided during the dark period of emergency the Supreme Court failed to protect the fundamental rights of Indian people during emergency when the judicial intervention was acutely needed. In the above case, the question arose whether the impugned dark law known as maintenance of internal security act (MISA) which took away the fundamental liberties of Indian people was valid? Whether fundamental rights of equality and fundamental freedom guaranteed under the Constitution could be suspended during emergency?

To the utter dismay of Indian people the Supreme Court by a majority vote decided that the only rule of law during emergency was the emergency law itself, and the judiciary including the Supreme Court will not inquire into the validity of a preventive detention even when it is made with malafide motives.

It is a matter of great regret that [barring two Hon'ble Justices, Mr. Justice H.R. Khanna and Mr. Justice A.C. Gupta], Indian Supreme Court failed Indian people during emergency when there was the dire need for the judicial intervention to protect Indian citizens against Governmental excesses.

(vi) Post-emergency, liberal interpretation of fundamental rights and relaxation of traditional standards of locus standi

Once the emergency was lifted and the dictatorial Government of Mrs. Indira Gandhi was defeated in 1977, due to committing atrocities on Indian people and depriving them of their freedom, the message was loud and clear that Indian people preferred freedom over bread. The Indian Supreme Court also started an era of liberal interpretation of fundamental rights. For example, in *Menaka Gandhi vs. Union of India (1978),* the Supreme Court gave a liberal interpretation to the term (liberty) and 'procedure established by law' under Article 21 of the Constitution. Rejecting the earlier narrow interpretation of A.K. Gopalan ruling, Justice Mr. Bhagwati observed that the term 'liberty' used in Article 21 of the Constitution is of the widest amplitude. It was further held that the term 'procedure established by law' will be interpreted as reasonable, fair and just procedure and not mere any procedure passed by competent legislature. In the present case, the passport of Menaka Gandhi was impounded by passport authorities without providing any reasonable opportunity of hearing. When she demanded as to why her passport was impounded the passport authority replied that it was done in 'public interest'. When she further insisted that what was the compelling public interest to impound her passport, the government replied that even the ground for impounding the passport could not be disclosed in 'public interest'. So she challenged the decision of the passport authority. The Supreme Court gave a liberal interpretation to Article 21 of the Constitution which provided that nobody could be deprived of his life or personal liberty except according to the procedure established by law. The Supreme Court held that only by a reasonable, just and fair procedure, the fundamental rights of a citizen could be curtailed.

The above liberal interpretation of the Supreme Court was followed in other cases. Not only this, the traditional standards of locus standi were also relaxed. Earlier only an affected party could approach the court. But now it was held that any public spirited person can also approach on behalf of a socially or economically disabled person to espouse the claim on behalf of such disabled person. This gave rise to the plethora of public interest litigation cases which we witness today and which have been partly responsible for the judicial activism of the Supreme Court in India.

(vii) The Supreme Court in search of its identity—Exploring the potential and limitation of its role (late 1980s)

After the expansive interpretation of fundamental rights during the late 1970s and early 1980s, the Supreme Court fluctuated from giving liberal interpretation to gain narrow interpretation. In some cases it will go out and make the policies like Shah Bano case introducing reforms in personal laws of Muslim and yet in another case it will curtail the expansive span of fundamental rights. By this exercise the Supreme Court explored its potential to intervene in the policy matters as well as acknowledging its limitation. It was a period of exploration, marked with lack of consistency regarding judicial approach to interventions in policy making.

(viii) Attaining the maturity and asserting its self-importance (mid 1990 s)

The Supreme Court through its activists judges like Mr. Justice Hon'ble Kuldeep Singh, started experiencing the importance of Supreme Court in Indian context. The remarkable cases of this period were:

Supreme Court Advocate on Record Association vs. Union of India (1993) where after negating the earlier primacy given to the Executive in the appointment of judges, the Supreme Court assigned the key role to the Chief Justice of India and asserted its own independence. Earlier in *S. P. Gupta vs. Union of India (1984),* the Supreme Court missed the opportunity of claiming its autonomy in the transfer of judges and role of the Chief Justice of India was given a secondary status to the Chief Executive. But now this mistake was corrected and the Supreme Court rightly claimed the primacy of the Chief Justice of India and Judges of Supreme Court in matters of appointment of judges and thus the Indian Supreme Court attained its maturity.

Another example of this judicial maturity and assertion of judicial role in exercise of power by the Executive in imposing President Rule on BJP run States after demolition of Ayodhya Mosque is reflected in *S.R. Bommai vs. Union of India (1993).* In this case the Hindu minded BJP Governments in several States were dismissed by the Congress led Central Government on the ground that the demolition of Ayodhya Mosque in a BJP run U.P. State Government amounted to failure of the State Government to run it as per the provisions of the Constitution. Not only the Government of State of U.P. led by BJP party was dissolved but the State Government of other States where BJP was in power were also dissolved and the President Rule was imposed. The validity of the same was challenged before the Supreme Court and the Supreme Court struck down the order of Presidential Rule in some States as arbitrary use of power by the Central Government. So it shows that the Indian Supreme Court has attained its maturity to intervene in political matters where there was the possibility of abuse of power by the Central Government.

Similarly, the Supreme Court did not hesitate to strike down the allotment of Petrol Pumps by Petroleum Minister and allotment of Houses to government servants on the basis of discretionary quota of the Minister for Housing. In Criminal Law, the Supreme Court ordered the Central Bureau of Investigation (CBI) to investigate into the alleged acceptance of Hawala Money by political leaders and report the progress to the Supreme Court directly, without allowing it to be influenced by political bosses. Likewise, under the crusading spirit of Justice Kuldeep Singh, Supreme Court ordered closure of more than 500 industries to save the environment.

From the above instances, it is quite clear that the Indian Supreme Court has finally attained its maturity and gained sufficient self-confidence to correct the mistakes of executive and legislative wings of the government and to act as protector of Fundamental Values of Indian Society.

(ix) Supreme Court in the 21st century—utilising its potential to the fullest extent and acknowledging its limitations

Like any mature individual, now the Supreme Court should be able to realise its potential and acknowledge its limitations. Here I would suggest that the Indian Supreme Court will have to take Indian context into account, and it has to evolve its own strategy suiting Indian conditions. To contrast, let me give an example from the American context first.

Discussing the same situation in American context, American Jurist John Ely of Harvard has propounded a thesis that generally, political process can be relied on to deliver goods in America but in two cases the political process may malfunction and in such situations, judiciary, particularly Supreme Court, should not hesitate to intervene.

(a) When dominant political party is trying to suppress or stifle the voices of weaker parties and thus preventing free market of ideas.

(b) Where discrete, insular minorities are not able to assert their free voice and they need special protection under the democratic process.

This was the position in American context but in Indian context democracy is not yet so highly developed that the political process may be relied upon. In India, democracy is still an aspiration rather than an achievement. Under such circumstances, an active role on the part of the judiciary particularly Supreme Court to protect the weak, is necessary. I recommend that in Indian conditions, whenever there is a competition between the Centre and the State then Supreme Court should favour the State unless there is compelling public interest to the contrary.

When there is a conflict between the State and the individual or group of individuals, then Supreme Court should favour the individual or group of individuals over the State.

Whenever there is a conflict between the government and the individual, again the Supreme Court should insist on the fairness of the procedure including transparency of the decision making process.

The above mentioned principles are suggested keeping in view the Indian context. There is another distinction which has to be kept in mind. I will call it the distinction between the primary responsibility of judiciary and the secondary responsibility of the judiciary. The primary responsibility of the judiciary is to ensure that all the laws of the country are properly made, fairly and impartially administered and they are interpreted wisely suiting to the situation. This is the primary responsibility and the judiciary should pay top attention to it. To cite only one example, it is the primary responsibility of the judiciary to see that all the proper opportunities are given to a person against whom any adverse order is passed affecting his life, liberty, dignity, property or reputation. The judiciary has to make sure that no innocent person is falsely implicated and if any person or authority does so, then a quick and effective punishment is meted out. Similarly, no culprit howsoever high or influential he may be, should escape his well deserved deserts. Another primary responsibility of the judiciary is to make sure that its orders are implemented promptly and those who defy or violate the court order is dealt with sternly and swiftly.

The Secondary responsibility of the judiciary is to make sure that all the policy decisions of the country are imbued with a sense of fairness and consistent with sound common sense. But since there can be more than one reasonable interpretation of the same, the judiciary should intervene in the fields assigned to other wings of the Government only when there is a manifest error or abuse of power. This is so because judiciary cannot be expected to solve all the problems of the country, but at the same time no Indian citizen should be left with the impression that there is no justice in this country anywhere.

In the ultimate analysis, it is not to be forgotten that judiciary is going to have only as high quality of the decision making as the persons who would be manning it. Not only this, one has to watch against the abuse of power or serious errors of judgement by judiciary itself. As American Chief Justice Mr. Justice Warren Burger used to say that it is not that American Supreme Court gives the best or the wisest judgement, it is only the final judgement. Above all we have to also keep in mind that the ultimate protectors of quality of life in any institution are the people themselves. Justice Learned Hand of America has rightly issued the following warning which I paraphrase as follows.

Often I wonder why people place so much trust in the Constitution or Laws or the Courts. This much trust in law or courts or Constitution is misplaced. I warn you, liberty lives in the hearts of people. If it lives there, no laws, no courts, no Constitution can take it away. But if the spirit of liberty dies in the hearts of the people, no laws, no courts, no Constitution can bring it back.

We have to keep the above-mentioned sagacious warning of Justice Hand in mind even in Indian context and we have to keep the spirit of liberty alive by judging the judges and their judgements because the Constitution of India has been adopted in the name of we, the people of India.

15

THE JUDICIAL SYSTEM IN A POST-COLONIAL DEMOCRACY: THE INDIAN EXPERIENCE

Aswini K. Ray

Among the decaying institutions of governance in India's post-colonial democracy, the judicial system still remains the residual hope for justice as the last court of appeal and, paradoxically, also the ultimate source of despair for its citizens. Popular perceptions of the judicial system, rather than legal sanctions, which is the critical index of the legitimacy of any institution in a democracy, is not particularly edifying for the self-esteem of its incumbents.

When the alleged criminal incarcerated for years in the dungeons of the Indian prisons without trial threw the unmentionable excremental missile at "Your honour" in Delhi's Tees Hazari Courts, he was passing his unsolicited judgement on the system in his own way. Similarly, when the Delhi editor recommended psychiatric treatment of the supreme court judges in the high tide of 'judicial activism', he was also pronouncing his judgement on the system in the way open to a journalist. Both were, predictably, punished for contempt of court.

But, the empirical reality remains uncontestable, that the two allied institutions of the system of justice in Republican India —the police and the judiciary— are popularly perceived as those to which only the most unfortunate citizens are condemned. Consequently, the powerful and the cunning have devised alternative sources of 'justice', insulated from the formal system. In fact, it is the parallel system of 'justice', along with the parallel economy, which is increasingly becoming the dominant component of the citizens' conflict-resolution and grievance-redressal mechanism. In this sense by default, the judicial system has become dialectically linked with the criminalised system of governance in modern India's anomic politics, reinforcing it and, affected by it, in a process of retrogressive symbiosis.

Yet, the tragedy of our times is the equally grim reality that there is little soul-searching from within the various components, of India's formal system of justice to suggest any imminent possibility of internal correctives to this abiding process of institutional atrophy. Like in most other institutions in India, only retired professionals missing out on the sine-cure post-retirement assignments, display a level of profound wisdom of the ills of their system, that remain unnoticed through much of their illustrious career-graphs. Yet, the ray of hope emerges from the fact, that in most conflict-situations the demand for an "impartial judicial inquiry", howsoever elusive otherwise, still remains a recurrent assertion within India's democratic discourse.

While this residual source of hope needs to be built-upon for institutional reforms, it is important to ensure that such informs are not imposed from outside.

Firstly, because there are not too many democratic institutions in the country, like the parliament, bureaucracy, media or the Academia which have remained unaffected by the pervasively criminalised political process to be able to provide the source for innovative reforms based on normative concerns. Secondly, any suggested innovations from outside the system is likely to be resented by the institutional incumbents as either inspired or inadequately informed or based on insensitivity. This is particularly true of the judicial system with the mindset of its incumbents rooted in the traditional liberal principle of "independence of the judiciary", even in our post-colonial version of democracy.

Under the circumstances, it may be prudent to critically analyse the judicial system through informed public debate based on micro-level empirical details, to encourage internal correctives for reforms. Such criticisms cannot be allowed to be stifled on the plea of the "independence of the judiciary". On the contrary, such informed criticism may humiliate the delinquents from within the system to suggest their own remedies for their ailments, thereby helping the process of internal corrective mechanism, and macro-level systemic reforms. There seems to be few alternatives options to provide remedies that are less perverse than the disease.

At any rate, the hallowed liberal principle of "independence of the judiciary" cannot be allowed to be delegitimised as an unjust instrument to protect the delinquent that constitute a significant component of all institutions of governance in modern India's post-colonial democracy. This component is particularly damaging for the legitimacy of the judicial system as the ultimate source of justice for the citizens. And, it would require a lot of nervous arrogance for anyone, including the "Lordships", to assume that in the all-encompassing anomie of the political process and institutional atrophy, the judicial system, as envisaged in the Republican Constitution, has remained an oasis of probity and rectitude, even "independence". In its own enlightened self-interest to reinforce the self-esteem of its incumbents, the judicial system must reciprocate the liberal principle of encouraging the innocence of the citizens to be able to say that "the Emperor is naked." That is the hope and spirit of the present exercise, restricted to underscoring some inadequacies viewed from outside, hoping to encourage solutions emerging from within the system.

In this context, three macro-level interrelated problems of the judicial system demand immediate remedial measures : (i) delayed justice; (ii) expensive justice; (iii) perverse justice. As for the first problem, the empirical reality speaks for itself, viz., there are now more than 20 million court cases pending in the various courts of the country. Cases in the national capital's lower courts take anything between three to eight years for judgements; and in the higher courts much the same, if not longer. The causes for such delayed justice are diverse, some less open to solutions than others which are relatively easy to resolve. For example, the problem of large-scale judicial vacancies could, and should, be relatively easily resolved by procedural streamlining of appointments and transfers. This is a managerial problem of systems organisation and procedure which could be resolved by seeking professional advice that abound in the private sector and regularly sought by the corporates to improve systemic efficiency. Similarly, transfers, particularly promotion of judges, could be linked to completion of their pending cases to reduce the recurrent problem of frivolous grounds for adjournment of hearings. In one case in Tees Hazari Court that we followed as part of an academic study, four adjournments spanning a period of three years was granted by the Rent Tribunal on the specious plea that the counsel's father was in a critical condition in the ICU of a hospital. In another case, as part of the same study, the counsel himself was supposed to be in the ICU, as claimed in his petition, while he was arguing his case in another court on the same day. In our research investigations, we were told that in all such cases, the onus of proof against such claims lay on the contesting counsel. And, by convention, the lawyers conveniently show the reciprocal 'courtesy' of not contesting each other's claims. Such cases of obvious ploy to prolong the judicial process to the unjust advantage of one party in any dispute, and the counsels on both sides, can be considerably reduced by simply shifting the obligatory onus of proof to the petitioner.

The more complex cause for delayed justice caused by recurrent lawyers' strikes could also be reduced by some financial costs made obligatory for the lawyers on strike to pay as part of their democratic obligations to the litigants, particularly the adversely affected party in any dispute, who becomes the unwitting victim of such strikes.

That would still leave out a large number of other causes for delayed justice in India for which remedial measures are more complex, in some cases impossible. For example, sudden illness of the judge, unanticipated holidays to mourn or celebrate myriad political and religious events, sudden general breakdown of law and order, fire, accidents, bomb blasts, epidemics and many other imponderables that constitute part of life in modern India. Even on many such cases, it may be possible to explore the threshold rule for a possible consensus among the various components of the judicial process. At any rate, for all courts, particularly at the lower levels, the number of judgements required to be delivered for any predetermined period to be decided by professional experience, ought to constitute an index of efficiency for purposes of promotions. Alternatively, transparent and quantifiable criteria of efficiency of Judges must emerge from the professionals within the system for career rewards, than simply seniority, as in most other professions.

The second macro-level problem of the system, that of expensive justice, could be considerably mitigated simply by speeding up the process; and through modern technological aids, like computerisation and reduction of the intermediaries between the clients and the judges. As for the two main components of the cost of justice, consisting of the court and lawyer's fees, both need some rationalisation and monitoring. While it may be useful to explore extending the system of *Amicus-Curie* beyond its present scope, the possibilities of more direct communications between the litigants and the judges, without the intervention of lawyers, needs positive encouragement from within the system; systemic reforms to facilitate the process by simplifying the procedures of litigation could be explored.

But most important, lawyers' fees at all levels have to be fixed by their respective Bar Councils and ought to be clearly mentioned in all petitions transacted through any lawyer in courts. Equally important would be to make it obligatory to provide the Income Tax PAN for all lawyers as a precondition for their registration for professional license. As an important component of the legal system of justice the legal profession must be obliged to establish its own credentials of conforming to the obligation of submitting regular tax returns.

The problem of perverse justice is more complex, and require more wide-ranging and informed debate for measure to stem the rot. While landmark judgements of the higher courts receive their due media attention sparking off public debates, the overwhelming component of judicial verdicts in the country affecting the citizens, consisting of judgements in the lower courts, howsoever perverse, receive little public notice. Since it would be a little illogical to assume that wisdom varies directly with the pecking order of the judicial structure, it may be worthwhile to explore measures to encourage informed public debates on Lower Court judgements without the threat of "contempt of court". Any system operated by fallible homosapiens in its own enlightened interest of legitimacy, must be open to the corrective of the democratic process. In the US, the "judicial tyranny" of the pre-"New Deal" era, emerging from the "due process" clause of the constitution, had to be undermined by the charismatic Roosevelt's stick-and-carrot populist politics. In India, the phase of "Judicial Activism" also led to its predictable judicial excesses even at the highest levels of the system. At lower levels, they constitute an abiding existential reality at the cost of justice to large section of its citizens. For example, we found in our study, one verdict in a Rent Court stipulated that a single girl-child of an old widower had no business to provide for the father's accommodations, because her primary obligations was to "look after her in-laws". We were told the appeal against the verdict is pending in the High Court for the last five years while the septuagenarian father living in rented accommodation is slowly sinking from old age ailments. Even in the higher courts, when the policemen who murdered Dr. Ramanathan, the pediatrician of the poor, in broad daylight in Warangal; or the murderers of Trade Unionist Sankar Guha Niyogi, or student leader Chandrasekhar, or Delhi's ghastly "Tandoor" murderer, remain unpunished, either because of political or money power or the inadequacy of the legal system, the legitimacy of the system itself, and the self-esteem of its incumbents, is bound to be undermined in popular perceptions.

If the system feels threatened to open itself to the floodgates of public criticism even against its delinquents, it must evolve internal mechanisms to acknowledge and reward judgements at all levels that reinforce the legitimacy of the judicial system, and punish the aberrants. Alternatively, it must risk the periodic humiliation from desperate undertrials like the one at Tees Hazari mentioned earlier.

But most important, is to evolve ways of attracting the talented and the motivated to the profession and provide periodic in-service training and Refresher course as obligatory preconditions for career advancements as in any other profession. As of now, the judiciary is probably the only institutions in India where career rewards up to the highest level is based only on 'eminence' as perceived by the appointing authority. Consequently, periodic controversy around appointments undermine the moral authority of the incumbents and legitimacy of the system.

As of now, except some who are attracted to it as part of family professions, the bulk of the recruits to the entire legal profession—and through it to the benches till the highest level—are drawn from the dregs and drop-outs from the university system as the last resort of self-employment. Within the anomic political process, they soon rise up the ladder of success through the operation of "Greschami's Law" that is unavoidable in an open anarchic system of freewheelers that puts a premium on such normless talents.

For example, we found that a relatively low-profile Law Minister in the Union Cabinet survived at least four different Prime Ministers successive portfolio reshuffles without either himself being an eminent jurist or a political heavyweight. When Mrs. Indira Gandhi, for example demanded the "commitment" of the judiciary at the highest level in the country, except one superseded judge, the entire Supreme Court not only accepted it without protest, but one of "His Lordships" actually accepted its logical rewards. Such scenario cannot legitimise the liberal principle of "judicial independence", much less help to reinforce it. The system ought to devise mechanism to attract self-respecting talents to the profession to reinforce its collective self-esteem and professional ethics, and consequent popular legitimacy.

This is important also in the context of one of the the major macro-level problems of India's post-colonial democracy, viz., the increasing deliberalisation of the democratic structure manifested through four principal trends across the board, and cutting across the political divide in the country : (i) the increasing constriction of citizens' Fundamental Rights as guaranteed by the Republican constitution through successive amendments; (ii) abiding continuity if the "Preventive Detention" clause in different forms; (iii) Rule by Executive Ordinances as a substitute for legislative enactment's; (iv) proliferation of new repressive legislation's along with new coercive instruments of governance, like police, intelligence and paramilitary institutions.

In this process, the role of the judiciary has complemented Executive Authoritarianism. Paradoxically, the judiciary even at the highest level, has generally asserted strident independence when the Executive authority has been weak,—as during unstable coalitions—led by minority governments, while it has been less assertive of its "independence" against strong Executive authority; it virtually capitulated to the Emergency regime by its endorsement of the 42nd Constitutional Amendment. Paradoxically, it is in time of such powerful Executive authority threatening citizens' rights that the judicial system remains the only hope as the last court of appeal; while weak executives offer many alternative political options for redress within the democratic structure. Also, periods like the Emergency in India provide the occasions to test the institutional legitimacy of the judicial system. That is the sense in which the Allahabad High Court Judge who declared Prime Minister Indira Gandhi's election as null and void for "corrupt practices" or Justice Khanna who resigned in protest against his supercession still remain cult-figures in popular imagination rather than Justice Ray who cashed on his "commitment" to Executive authority. It is in this context also that the periodic debates in India around the Parliament vs. Judiciary as the more credible protector of the citizens' Fundamental Rights appear somewhat banal in popular imagination, and at the cost of the legitimacy of the Judicial system.

The much-hyped phase of 'Judicial Activism' in Indian politics in recent times need to be contextualised within these broad contours of the aforementioned popular perception. While the only new Right granted to the citizen in Republican India, in the form of the Right of Public Interest Litigation, has emerged from the Judicial system, rather than the Parliament, it is also uncontestable that in the subterranean process of de-liberalisation of the democratic structure, the judiciary has been an accomplice of both Executive Authoritarianism and majority tyranny. That is why 'Judicial Activism', despite the initial excitement, leading to predictable populist excesses, soon became mired in controversy and lost its steam.

The situation is full of new challenges, and some hope. The decaying system still periodically spawns surprises, and occasional individual judges as role-models of juridical rectitude without making any significant dent to the credibility of the system. Like about most other democratic institutions of modern India, whatever one generalises, the contrary is also true. This duality between the operational and the dysfunctional, which characterise all Indian institutions is most damaging for the judicial system. Adjudication becomes perverse oppression when exercised by individuals with questionable credentials within an institutional system with weak popular legitimacy.

16

EVOLUTION OF CONCEPT OF SOCIAL JUSTICE AND JUDICIAL ACTIVISM

Puja Khattar

In recent years, a new expression, resurgence of "judicial activisim" has attracted the attention of social scientists, politicians and lawyers. The developments in India during the last two to three years, particularly after a number of judgements by the judiciary have been pronounced on social justice, corruption, atrocities on women, environment, etc., have generated a new interest on the role of judiciary in the Indian political system and its constitution. Before we examine, the important role which the judiciary has played in the evolution of concept of social justice let us look at the problem from another angle.

The most obvious contrast between India and Pakistan is of course the one that pertains to the political fortunes of the two countries. Except for the brief period of eighteen months between June 1975 and January 1977, the period of emergency, India has managed to sustain a secular democratic system of government on a scale unparalleled in the world. This achievement is all the more remarkable in view of the fact that India's democratic system has been nurtured under conditions usually thought to be inimical to democracy: a vast, mostly illiterate, population; an area which, although larger than the US, in most parts still has extremely poor means of regular communication; a great diversity of religions, sects, cultures and languages, often in conflict with one another; an *overwhelming rural sector still* caught in ancient social relations, customs and ways of thinking, and so on. Despite all this, a democratic system has not only been established in the length and breadth of India, it has withstood some profound shocks, both internal and external. For example, hardly had the country the time to pull itself together after the trauma and turmoil of the partition days of 1947 when it had to face the barely concealed Pakistani invasion of Kashmir and the eventual loss of a portion of its territory to that country; then came the language riots of the fifties, which created a constitutional crisis just two years after India had proudly proclaimed its Constitution; this was followed by the Chinese invasion in 1962, the wars with Pakistan, the widespread communal riots, the challenges from extremist Sikhs and the military operation in the Golden Temple, the assassination of Mrs. Indira Gandhi and most recently of Rajiv Gandhi. Any of these crises could have provided a pre-text for the suspension of the democratic order or for military intervention in the affairs of the state. However, India's democracy survived all these challenges.[1]

Equally remarkable is the fact that although the Indian National Congress and especially Jawaharlal Nehru had been passionately attached to the concept of a strongly centralised government—partly as a result of the deep fears of the "balkanisation" of the country in the wake of partition; partly because of an ideological confusion, itself the product of feudal social relations, which equates unity with centralisation of power and nationhood with ethnic and cultural uniformity; and partly because of the dogma that only centralisation of resources and management can carry through a programme of industrialisation and modernisation in a backward country—under popular pressure, they allowed new states to be created within a space of fourteen years (1952-66) along linguistic and even religious lines. The central government, whatever authoritarian reaction it might have displayed at first to the minority nations demands for separate homelands, did not in the end crush their aspiration by resorting to the argument that such demands would jeopardise the integrity or security of the country.[2] In the history of nations such flexibility on the part of those who hold power is rather rare. Indeed, Indian democracy has proved resilient enough to accommodate even communist state governments within its overall system (Kerala, West Bengal and Tripura)—a fact that puts it high above the models of pluralist democracy in the West. In the late 90s, Indian political system has entered a new phase of coalition governments, if one goes by recent developments, no single party can monopolise power.

Seen in this context, the Judiciary in India has begun to assume a new importance.

A noisy, needless and nugatory controversy was raised sometime ago on one issue which affect our judiciary and judicial system. This related to the role of a judge in terms of his milieu. This issue was partially solved on the basis of the concept that judiciary has to interpret the various laws in terms of the basic postulates of the Constitution. In fact the various judgements of the judiciary have given a new content to the Indian judicial system.

It is significant to mention that in the United States of America when Franklin Delano Roosevelt was elected on the New Deal platform all his great purposes for economic justice stood threatened by a conservative Supreme Court. President Roosevelt made it clear beyond the shadow of a doubt that if the Court did not change, he would change the Court. The new deal went through and the Court went along with it. It would be idle to question the democratic bonafides of President Roosevelt or the United State itself in consequence.[3]

The 14th amendment to the US Constitution gives us a supreme example of how a measure designed for one purpose can be thwarted, negated or fulfilled by different interpretations over time by different judges with different outlooks. This amendment guaranteeing equal protection of the laws was designed to benefit emancipated Negroes. It was, however, used precisely for the opposite purpose as a shield against social legislation in the early decades of this century by judges who held to a laissez-faire philosophy and invalidated a number of social and economic measures. The powerful dissenting opinions of Justices Holmes and Brandies who shared a different and liberal outlook in those times laid the foundations for future redress. Thus in the 50's this same measure was interpreted by a new set of judges to serve its real purpose as a barrier to racial discrimination. Led by Justice Earl Warren a series of landmark decisions were handed down by the US Supreme Court earning for Warren applause as a courageous leader seeking to adapt legal rules to modern conditions in the light of moral considerations.[4]

The Constitution of India has been regarded as less of a constitutional document and more of a unique charter of human emancipation through economic and social justice. It would be totally wrong to suggest that it was originally devised to perpetuate bondage from which the nation had just emerged. Refashioned over the years, the single-minded intention has been to perfect it into a true instrument and vehicle of liberty and progress for the masses of the Indian people and not for a small elitist and predatory minority. The role of the judge in reflecting this motivation and impulse was manifest, regardless of who was the ruling power and what its ruling ideology.

As early as 1957 when he joined the Supreme Court, Justice Gajendragadkar may be said to have delivered the first of a series of blows on behalf of social justice. Handling down judgment in a case that year he expounded the welfare state ideals of the Indian Constitution and its guiding principles of social welfare and common good. The State he said, is no longer content to play the part of a passive onlooker in an industrial dispute. The old principle of the absolute freedom of contract and the doctrine of laissez-faire have yielded place to new principles of social welfare and common good.

From then on through 1966 when he retired as Chief Justice of India he delivered a series of judgements in landmark cases to uphold the principles of social justice. A very telling and emphatic assertion of these principles is to be found in a 1963 judgement where he says:

In our opinion, the argument that the considerations of social justice are irrelevant and untenable in dealing with industrial disputes, has to be rejected without any hesitation. The development of industrial law during the last decade and several decisions of this Court in dealing with industrial matters have emphasised the relevance, validity and significance of the doctrine of social justice. Indeed the concept of social justice has now become such an integral part of industrial law that it would be idle for any party to suggest that industrial adjudication can or should ignore the claims of social justice in dealing with industrial disputes. The concept of social justice is not narrow, one-sided, or pedantic, and is not confined to industrial adjudication alone. Its sweep is comprehensive. It is founded on the basic ideal of socio-economic equality and its aim is to assist the removal of socio-economic disparities and inequalities; nevertheless, in dealing with industrial matters, it does not adopt a doctrinaire approach and refuses to yield blindly to abstract notions, but adopts a realistic and pragmatic approach. It, therefore, endeavours to resolve the competing claims of employers and employees by finding a solution which is just and fair to both parties with the object of establishing harmony, between capital and labour, and good relationship.

The concept of law being directed towards social change and the strengthening of national unity, to create a new social and economic order devoid of injustices and exploitation were inherent in the democratic structure that the leaders of freedom movement visualised.

All over the world it is being increasingly recognised that law is not merely a means of enforcing static authority but an expression of man's wisdom and self-discipline through which societies can resolve their internal anomalies and improve their capacity to meet the challenge of time.

In a fast-changing social and economic order, law cannot remain immutable: it must change with changing needs of the time to subserve the national interest.

Our Constitution aims at the realisation of social and economic justice in a framework of liberty. It is a character of change, not an apologia for status quo. A living Constitution cannot bind down future generations. No human institution can survive if it resists the future. While upholding basic values, the law must enable political institutions to be resilient and responsive to a new situation.

The demand that the law must change in order to realise the aspirations of the people, particularly the poor and oppressed, has been voiced by the National Forum of Lawyers Conferences to press the demand that the law must promote national unity, secularism, preserve and strengthen sovereignty and integrity of the country.

The Indian Constitution is first and foremost a social document. The fundamental rights and the directive principles had their roots deep in the struggle for independence and they were included in the Constitution in the hope and expectation that one day the tree of true opportunity would bloom in India.

Merely inscribing high ideals and objectives in a country's constitution is no guarantee that socio-economic objectives would be automatically attained. It is up to the legal profession more than any other section of society to quicken the pace of socio-economic change. It is for them to become social engineers and build a new desirable social structure out of the shambles left behind by an iniquitous system.[5]

Since the very inception of our Constitution we have committed ourselves to the concept of Rule of Law, Welfare State and Justice in all forms. The quest of human race for justice in all its forms is manifested throughout during the struggle of mankind in the long history of civilization. The idea of providing justice to every person in need cannot be realised fully until such time as legal assistance is made available to the more indigent sections of our society. As long as human instincts dominate human actions, conflcts are inevitable. The Courts of law are temples of justice where justice is to be dispensed without any fear or favour; without any distinction between the rich and the poor; the advanced and the downtrodden; protected and the unprotected. To provide legal assistance to those who cannot afford is not merely a social obligation, but has also become a State obligation at the present time. It is heartening to note that all the concerned, the Government the Bench and the Bar who command a privileged position in our political system, have started paying maximum attention to provide assistance to the poor in the vital field of legal advice which touches every aspect of life of a common man. Equality of law and equal protection of laws guaranteed under the Constitution cannot achieve the purpose unless protection by the Courts is afforded to the poorest amongst the poor. That would be translating into reality what Magna Carta professed; to no one deny or delay the right of justice.

What is of far reaching relevance after 50 years of independence is that political freedom cannot be, and is not, an end in itself. The Preamble of the Constitution has declared that our country is determined and dedicated to the task of establishing justice political, social and economic and the subject of the Indian Democracy is to create a new social order. It is only when this dream is realised that the objectives laid down in the Constitution will be redeemed.

Fifty years have passed since India won independence and these years have, no doubt, been momentous and eventful. The nation has faced dangers and conquered them. The nation has made progress in socio-economic matters. But, judged by the yardstick of the objectives of the Constitution, the progress is slow and naturally millions of our countrymen, who live in villages and smaller places, feel frustrated and angry that the promise of giving them social and economic justice still remains to be fulfilled. Laws have been passed covering socio-economic needs of the country, but many of them have not been fully implemented and the implementation of some others has been totally inadequate. Untouchability, still continues to govern the lives of a section of our society; poverty still stalks abroad; unemployment is faced by many people both educated and uneducated; communal differences and suspicions have not been banished, and the Indian community as a whole still continues to be a fragmented traditional community which, loves to look back and leans on tradition rather than look forward and lean on reason. The growing impatience, frustration and anger of large masses of this country poses a very serious challenge to the progress of Indian democracy.

If, however, these problems are not speedily, effectively, honestly, and wisely solved, anger and frustration which are writ large in the eyes of hundreds of people will burst into an explosion. As is well-known hunger makes men angry and angry, men know no reason. We should bear this aspect in mind in discussing the problem of lawyers obligations in a changing society.

At this stage, it would not be inappropriate to emphasise the relevance and significance of the three major articulate postulates of our Constitutions. The first major articulate postulate is that the framers of the Constitution were conscious that political freedom, which the country had won, cannot be an end in itself; but to the teeming millions of the country, political freedom meant only a means to the betterment of their lot, and its ultimate goal must be to afford to every citizen of the country full and fair opportunity to enjoy life, liberty and happiness; and the full enjoyment of life necessarily involves the principle that political freedom has no significance for the masses unless it gives them economic justice. In other words, social equality and economic justice are the ultimate, if not the immediate, objectives of Indian democracy.

This aspect needs to be underlined because this Indian political elite irrespective of its ideology is getting isolated from the common people.

The second major postulate relates to that part of the Constitution which deals with Fundamental Rights and Directive Principles of State Policy. Whereas Fundamental Rights guaranteed by the Constitution, the most distinguishing feature of Indian democracy; the Directive Principles enshrined in the Constitution, the corner-stone and indeed, the Magna Carta of economic Justice. The fact that Directive Principles, though fundamental to the governance of the country, were not made justiceable, does not detract from the place of pride which they occupy in the scheme of national life contemplated by the Constitution. The service of India, means the service of the millions who suffer. It means the ending of poverty and ignorance and disease and inequality of opportunity. The ambition of the greatest men of our country has been to wipe every tear from every eye. That may be beyond us, but as long as there are tears and suffering so long our work will not be over.

The third major postulate is that the framers of the Constitution were aware that as Indian democracy makes progress towards establishing social and economic justice, the hopes and aspirations of the have-nots and the underprivileged as well as the backward classes and economically weaker sections of the community will expand and laws, and even the Constitution, may have to be amended in order to meet the challenge of the expanding horison of the growing just legitimate and unsatisfied hopes and aspirations of the common men, knowing, as they did, that the framework of fundamental rights particularly the right to property may need to be modified, they conferred on Parliament unambiguious and specific power to amend the Constitution. Indeed the scheme of fundamental rights guaranteed by Article 19 read with its provisions expressly shows that fundamental rights were not intended to be absolute and were, from the very commencement, subject to the limitations prescribed by the respective provisos. Even so, Article 368 conferred plenary constituent powers on Parliament to amend the Constitution. The significance of the words plenary constituent powers must be clearly borne in mind. The powers are constituent and not ordinary legislative powers and they are plenary and not subject to any limitations except the procedural limitations prescribed by Article 368.

Therefore, the third major postulate which we have to bear in mind is that the framers of the Indian Constitution have deliberately and wisely conferred on Parliament plenary constituent powers to amend the Constitution according to the requirements of the times. The governing consideration in this matter would naturally be the felt necessities of the times which are bound to change from generation to generation in the case of a country which is committed to the abolition of poverty and the establishment of social equality and economic justice.

The functional jurisprudence looks upon law as an instrument of social change. This philosophy about the function of law has been very eloquently expanded by the great law teacher, Dean Roscoe Pound. According to him: "the sociological method consists in study of a legal system functionally, as a social instrument, as a part of social control, and study of its institutions, doctrines and precepts with respect to the social ends to be served". It presupposes that law is a specialized agency of social control. According to this view, law has to meet the challenge of the times from epoch to epoch. As Pound further observes: "While jurists have been at these tasks, a new social order has been building which makes new demands and presses upon the legal order with a multitude of unsatisfied desires. Once more we must build rather than merely improve; we must create rather than merely order and systematise and logically reconcile details". According to the vision of Pound, legal history is the record of a continually wider recognising and satisfying human wants or claims or desires through social control; a more embracing and more effective securing of social interests; a continually more complete and effective elimination of waste and precluding friction in human enjoyment of the goods of existence—in short, a continually more efficacious social engineering.[6]

A national debate on 'Whither the Judicial Revolution?' is on the urgent though stagnant agenda of the Republic because law, justice, and Courts have a reach over everyone from the womb to the tomb, and enjoy a power over citizens' life, liberty and property, too large to be left to men in robes lettered mainly in law.

Freedom brought in its wake expectations, but as decades drifted, expectations darkened and tended to explode. If there be nothing for the long-forsaken to look for from the law there may be something for them to shoot for against that law, is a time-bomb caveat.[7]

This brings us to the conclusion that in a period, when the political structures in India are undergoing transformation and the concept of social justice still is vaguely defined, the judiciary has come to occupy strategic position in the entire structure of our society—legislature, judiciary and executive. The old political formations are either in the process of decay or changing. The new political formations have yet to clearly define their concept of social justice. In such a situation, judiciary and judicial verdicts perhaps will play an important role in the coming period in enriching and concrertising the basic concepts of social justice as enshrined in our Constitution.

Laws are meant to fit existing conditions, and they are meant to help us to better ourselves. If conditions, change how can the old laws fit in? They must change with changing conditions, or else they become iron chains keeping us back while the world marches on. No law can be an unchangeable law. It must be based on knowledge, and as knowledge grows, it must grow with it.

It would thus be clear that our founding fathers were fully conscious about the dynamic role which law had to play in assisting Indian democracy to achieve the goal of establishing socio-economic justice in our country. They knew that democracy can hope to achieve its objective only with the help of law and so, they legitimately anticipated that the Indian Legislatures will be wise in passing laws which will meet the challenge of poverty, hunger, unemployment, squalor, disease, as well as social obscurantism and ignorance. They also believed that, once these laws are passed, they would be fully implemented; and they fondly hoped that the Indian judiciary, in interpreting these laws, will adopt a constructive approach and take into account the felt necessities of the times.

In a democratic country committed to the task of establishing socio-economic equality, the centre of gravity of law is not so much Legislatures, though the Legislatures pass the law; nor Court-rooms, though Judges interpret the laws and consider their validity; nor the chambers of jurists, though the jurists formulate principles of Jurisprudence which guide the Legislatures and help the Judges. The centre of gravity of law lies basically in the unsatisfied but legitimate hopes and aspirations of the common citizens of the country.[8]

REFERENCES

1. Iqbal Khan, *Fresh Perspectives on India and Pakistan*, pp. 1-2.
2. *Ibid.*, pp. 2-3.
3. Dr. P.B. Gajendragadkar, *Law, Lawyer and Social Change*, p. xi.
4. *Ibid.*, p. xii.
5. *Ibid.*, pp. xiii, xvi-xvii.
6. *Ibid.*, p. 24.
7. Justice V.R. Krishna Iyer, *Perspectives in Criminology: Law and Social Change*, pp. 97-98.
8. Dr. P.B. Gajendragadkar: op.cit., p. 26.

17

POLITICS OF JUSTICE

K.P.S. Gill

> "When I use a word," Humpty Dumpty said, in rather a scornful tone, "it means just what I choose it to mean—neither more nor less."
>
> "The question is," said Alice, "whether you can make words mean so many different things."
>
> "The question is," said Humpty Dumpty, "which is to be master—that's all."[1]

In a surprisingly candid statement, Justice M. N. Venkatachaliah, former Chief Justice of India, and presently the Chairman of the National Human Rights Commission, recently declared, "The judiciary is becoming formidable and asserting its place under the sun."[2] This was, perhaps, the clearest and most unambiguous description, by a member of the superior judiciary itself, of an aspect of India's judicial evolution over the past two decades; an aspect that law academics in the early eighties spoke of as 'jurisdiction hunger'; an aspect that has transformed itself in the late nineties into nothing less than a jurisdictional rampage.

The essence of this evolution, so eloquently expressed by Justice Venkatachaliah, is the contest for power between different arms of government; a contest that the Constitution of India had already settled half a century ago, but which has been thrown open once again by widespread political irresponsibility and by legislative incompetence. Today, as new areas of 'legislative infirmity' are discovered by activist courts, as the power vacuum consequent upon executive failure and corruption is exposed, the judiciary has expanded its sphere of activities and influence and, indeed, become 'formidable'. This development has, by and large, met with public applause and adulation as the common man—supported by the enthusiastic, if uncritical media—has come to believe, in an atmosphere of pervasive political uncertainty and administrative chaos, that the judiciary is his only saviour.

Among those who share this conviction, however, you will find a surprisingly small number of litigants. The fact of the matter is that, in its quest for 'a place in the sun', essentially a political quest, the judiciary has taken recourse to characteristically 'political' methods; and judicial populism has been the most successful among these. The essence of populism, however, is that it plays on public sentiments without addressing the essential issues of policy and performance that could alleviate public suffering. Thus, despite the enormous fanfare that has accompanied many recent decisions and a number of politically sensitive prosecutions [none of which has yet resulted in a conviction, excluding that of the ill-fated Kalpnath Rai—a decision which was swiftly overturned] the judicial record has not been particularly encouraging. For the over three crore litigants waiting for justice in various courts, some of them for several decades, the spectacle of a former Prime Minister being paraded before a criminal court, or the knowledge that the Supreme Court has now defined a code of sexual propriety in the workplace, is not necessarily gratifying.

Protected by the law of contempt, by the essentially closed nature of the judicial family, and by the general tendency of the public to be extremely deferential in their attitude towards the courts, the judiciary has succeeded in directing critical attention away from itself towards the failures of the other arms of government. There is, however, a growing realisation today that the judicial system and its machinery are straying from the Constitutional path and not performing their true function, a function the public has a right to expect them to perform. Despite the increasing exhibitionism of judicial processes, especially in 'Public Interest' litigation, the courts are no longer perceived as effective institutions for the resolution of conflict and for the administration of justice. Justice A.S. Anand of the Supreme Court stated recently that a victim of crime has only two options: to approach the police or the courts. "For him unfortunately," he confessed, "neither of the two is an attractive proposition. If he is hesitant to approach the police station for reasons which are by no means unknown, his reluctance to approach the court is also not without reason."[3]

Justice Anand characteristically fails to elaborate upon the reasons for the public's reluctance to approach the courts. The judiciary has consistently resisted any objective attempts to define reasonable criteria by which its performance is to be judged, even as it has placed itself beyond the scope of political or executive review.[4] But the reality is difficult to escape. "Most Supreme Court Judges," the eminent constitutional expert H.M. Seervai remarked, "live in a dream world of their own. There are rhetorical passages in a number of judgements as to the intellectual and moral qualities which judges should possess and, by implication, most of them do possess. In my submission, it is necessary to point out that this picture of qualities and character possessed by most Judges, and the further view that all High Court Judges are men of integrity and are incorruptible is not justified by matters on record."[5] Seervai then proceeds to quote an interview given by the late Chief Justice Venkataramiah a day before he retired; the excerpts from the interview are singularly edifying, and refer to Judges who "are willing to be 'influenced' by lavish parties and whisky bottles," and to the trend of close relatives of judges practising and influencing decisions in Courts where those judges were on the Bench.[6]

Today, it is not possible even to hold the view that the Supreme Court registry is beyond the shadow of corruption. It is not necessary, in this, to refer to the allegations of impropriety against the Chief Justice of India by a Judge of the Rajasthan High Court; or to the present allegations by a group of senior lawyers calling themselves the Committee for Judicial Accountability against the senior most puisne Judge of the Supreme Court. It is sufficient to note that at least one Judge of the Supreme Court, Justice V. Ramaswami, was found to have committed gross financial irregularities.

Despite the immaculate projections of members of the judiciary, it is clear that no institution can escape the influence of pervasive social and political vice. As Lord Devlin expressed it, *"on the whole* judges are not better than the society in which they live. When Ministers accepted bribes, Judges accepted bribes; when Ministers sold public offices, Judges sold public offices; when Ministers used public money on condition that they paid it back, Judges used public money on condition that they would pay it back."[7]

An institution, however, is not to be judged by the possibility of corruption within it, or by allegations of corruption against its individual members. No institution can obviate all such contingencies. An institution must be judged, rather, by its responses to evidence of corruption. Today, even as the Supreme Court spearheads a veritable crusade against corruption in all other arms of government, its response to evidence of corruption within the judicial fraternity is, to say the least, distinctly inconsistent.

I shall refer to an incident in this context, regarding which I have sufficient detail. In 1993, there was great commotion in Chandigarh over a speech at a meeting of the Punjab and Haryana High Court Bar Association in honour of the then Chief Justice of India, Justice M.N. Venkatachaliah [whom we have encountered above, celebrating the judiciary's "place in the sun"]. Present at the meeting, in addiction to the CJ, were four other Judges of the Supreme Court—Justice J.S. Verma [the former Chief Justice], Justice Kuldip Singh, Justice M.M. Punchhi and Justice A.S. Anand (present Chief Justice) as well as the Chief Justices of Rajasthan, Gujarat, Himachal Pradesh and Jammu & Kashmir, as also the Chief Justice and the Judges of the Punjab and Haryana High Court. The then Law Minister H. R. Bharadwaj was also present. Anupam Gupta, a member of the Bar Association, a prominent lawyer, and a legal columnist, was one of the speakers before this august gathering. I quote him at some length:[8]

> No system of justice, it has been said, can rise above the ethics of those who administer it.... When abuse of judicial power outgrows individual aberrations and

> becomes an institutional lifestyle, when judicial corruption ceases to be a mere rumour and develops into a universal perception, when judges scramble for ministerial favours and perks and State governments and Chief Ministers acquire greater clout over the Court than the Court has over them under the Constitution... it becomes a moral and Constitutional imperative to take action, in the celebrated words of President Roosevelt, to "save the Constitution from the Court and the Court from itself.

These were harsh words, but they were followed up with some hard numbers.

> As many as 14 out of 28 sitting Judges of the Punjab and Haryana High Courts, i.e., half of its total strength, have their close relatives practising in the High Court. Eight out of these 14 judges have more than one relative practising here. Over and above them, wards of two sitting Supreme Court Judges also practise in the High Court, one of them having more than one ward.

Gupta also referred to a Karnataka High Court judgement regarding the right and wrong of a judge's wife who was practising in the High Court where her husband was a judge; the Court observed:

> Many of the litigants in this Court are common men who would not be wrong in assuming that the learned counsel while sharing her connubial felicity may also share with the learned Judge her professional life.

Confronted with such allegations, there are only two possibilities, and two responsible courses of action available. Either the allegations were false, in which case, it was not only within the rights and the powers of the Supreme Court and High Court judges present there to proceed against and punish the speaker, but was their bounden duty in order to restore the reputation of the High Court; or there was substance in the allegations, in which case, after due investigation, corrective action should have been initiated to cleanse the Court of the evident taint on its reputation. What was the actual response?

All the judges of the Supreme Court and of the various High Courts, as well as the Law Minister walked out of the meeting 'in protest' against the speech. No action was taken on the allegations and, a deafening silence has since been maintained on the issues raised. In this context, it has, I think, been correctly remarked: "Sometimes silence is not golden—just yellow."[9]

A more recent example provides even greater illumination.

Since September 17, 1996, a criminal complaint has been pending in the court of the Chief Judicial Magistrate, Pali (Rajasthan), against Justice R.R. Jain, then a judge of the Gujarat High Court. According to the complaint, the judge engineered the wrongful arrest of a Pali advocate on false charges under the Narcotic Drugs and Psychotropic Substances Act, as also the advocate's subsequent release after he had agreed to vacate a shop where he had his office. The shop belonged to a family close to the judge, and the power of attorney for the family is held by the judge's uncle. At midnight on May 2, 1996, the Gujarat police handcuffed advocate Sumer Singh at Pali, and attempted to spirit him across the border to Palanpur in Gujarat. Fortunately for him, a patrol party of the Rajasthan police intercepted them and a record of events was created which the Gujarat police had not intended. The complaint states further that the judge arranged all this after attending a marriage in Pali at the house of the family that owned the disputed shop; he then travelled to Palanpur to meet his friend Sanjiv Rajendra Bhatt, the Superintendent of Police, Palanpur, and then proceeded to Ahmedabad to resume his duties in the High Court. Sumer Singh was falsely shown as having stayed in a hotel in Palanpur; recovery of opium was shown in his absence from the room he supposedly occupied. The Superintendent of Police then told him that the judge wanted the shop vacated, and if this was done, his release would be arranged. Otherwise the recovery of opium would be shown against him, and he would be prosecuted. The advocate's brother, a *tehsildar* and some others interceded with the judge, speaking to him over the phone, and eventually vacated the shop. On Sumer Singh's complaint, the Pali Bar Association wrote to the then Chief Justice of India, A.M. Ahmadi. In the absence of any response, the Gujarat Bar took notice, and passed a resolution against Justice R.R. Jain on June 22, 1996. Evidence against the judge in the form of transcripts of his tape-recorded conversation was available with advocates of the Pali Bar. Meanwhile, the Rajasthan police investigated the complaint and arrested the judge's uncle, Phootermal, and put him in jail. There has been no final report from the police on the complaint against the judge. Former Chief Justice J.S. Verma was reported to have been apprised of the case. R.R. Jain was then simply transferred from Gujarat to Madras as Additional Judge.[10] In this context, it must be recalled that, in the *Second Judges' Transfer Case,* Justice Verma, writing for the majority, had held that "Any transfer made on the recommendation of the Chief Justice is not to be deemed to be punitive...."[11] Nor would it be proper to have punitively transferred the judge without proper investigation of the case. Nor, indeed, can mere transfer be regarded as sufficient punishment for the very serious offences allegedly committed. Indeed, a grave question arises as to whether an individual charged with such an offence can or should be permitted to sit in judgement on others. Justice R.R. Jain, nevertheless, has now been recommended for confirmation as a permanent judge of the Madras High Court.

Can there be one law for judges, another for politicians and administrators, and still another for the common man?

The critical question, however, as with the decline of the other core institutions of democracy [the legislature and the executive], is not about corruption. It is about the effectiveness of these institutions in fulfilling the objectives of their constitution. Quantitative comparisons are, of course, impossible in this context, but the failure of the judiciary in this regard is no less dramatic than that of the other branches of government. To begin with the highest echelons of judicial leadership, Seervai has noted that "...with rare exceptions the standard of Supreme Court decisions has continued to fall steeply in matters involving questions of Constitutional Law...Judicial incompetence takes the form of ignorance of the legislative history; ignorance of the provisions of the Constitution; ignorance or disregard of well-settled principles of interpretation; ignorance of the meaning of ordinary English words; inability to draw correct conclusions from passages cited; and begging the question to be proved."[12] Seervai also speaks of the "disconcerting unpredictability of the Supreme Court"[13] as judges display tendencies to ignore precedent and established rules of Constitutional interpretation, operating not on accepted Constitutional, jurisprudential and judicial norms, but with each one "paddling his own canoe" [to borrow the phrase of Chief Justice Taft of the American Supreme Court].

It is in this tendency that we discover the essence of the breakdown of the adversary system of justice that we have inherited. Today, a veritable Babel of contradictory voices emanates from the Supreme Court as each judge actively intervenes to impose his personal 'philosophy' and political worldview on every controversy. Anglo-Saxon jurisprudence, the basis of our own judicial system, assigns an unambiguous role for the judiciary as an independent and disinterested arbiter between two [or more] adversaries, who agitate their claim before it; claims based on the law and laid down by the legislature. In criminal matters, one of the adversaries is invariably the state. The judiciary is required, however, to treat both the state and the accused on the same platform. Lord Denning explained the role of the judge in this system with great felicity:

> The judge's part in all this is to hearken to the evidence, only himself asking questions of witnesses when it is necessary to clear up any point that has been overlooked or left obscure; to see that the advocates behave themselves seemly and keep to the rules laid down by law; to exclude irrelevancies and discourage repetition; to make sure by wise intervention that he follows points that the advocates are making and can assess their worth; and at the end make up his mind where the truth lies. If he goes beyond this, he drops the mantle of a judge and assumes the robe of an advocate; and the change does not become him well. Lord Chancellor Bacon spoke right when he said that: "Patience and gravity of hearing is an essential part of justice; and an over-speaking judge is no well-tuned cymbal."[14]

Seervai describes the 'judicial temper' as:

> A frame of mind which is open till both sides have had their legitimate say but is decisive when both sides have been fully heard. Secondly, judicial temper also involves a frame of mind which decides each case on its merits and does not start with prepossessions in favour of one class or other.... A judge who closes his mind before he has heard both sides, and makes it clear that he supports one side, will talk a good deal to make his view prevail.[15]

Unfortunately, we are overwhelmingly confronted, today, with the phenomenon of the 'much-talking judge'[16] as courts take *suo motu* cognisance of matters, 'direct' investigative agencies to make inquiries and 'monitor' and 'supervise' the investigation—all in the interests of 'justice', of course. In this the lines of demarcation between judge and petitioner, or judge and complainant, decreed by the rule of law are all but obliterated as the court increasingly takes on the role of the prosecution. Apart from going against the basic character of our justice system, this also raises serious questions of equality before law. By such interventions courts direct the resources of the state towards a particular investigation—and, in many recent cases, in view of the court's interest this becomes disproportionate, often putting the defendant at an unfair disadvantage. More importantly, such interventicn sends confused signals to the subordinate judges who must eventually hear the case and give a verdict. In a case where the prosecution has been 'supervised' and 'monitored' by the Supreme Court [or even the High Court], it will be a brave judge indeed who would go against the prosecution; and the formal declaration by the superior court that the subordinate court must try the case "according to law" and ignore any observations the superior judges may have made does little to improve the subordinate judge's frame of mind. This is against the very basic tenets of natural justice, a denial of fair trial, and hence unconstitutional.

The 'much-talking judge' does irreparable harm both to the dignity of the court and to the cause of justice. It is not only subordinate courts, but advocates and investigators who are pressured by the views and antipathies that the judge may seek to impose on a particular case; where important interests of state or prominent personalities are involved, moreover, in pre-judging a case the judge seriously and permanently undermines the prospects of justice. We discover a process of a search for a preconceived 'truth', in which conclusions leap far ahead of 'facts', and what are construed as facts run well beyond the available evidence. In the *Punjab Mass Cremations* case, for instance, Justice Kuldip Singh, on the basis of nothing more than an unsubstantiated newspaper report, and well before any evidence regarding the alleged 'illegal' cremation of 1,000 unidentified bodies by the Punjab Police had been placed on record, declared in open court that the alleged incident was 'worse than genocide'.[17] The case is *sub judice* and it would be improper to go into the merits of subsequent investigations and proceedings; but the media accepted and splashed the Supreme Court judge's verbal *obiter dicta* as a final indictment of the Punjab Police, as a final judgement on its mode of functioning in the decade-long battle against terrorism.

What is possibly worse, is that Justice Kuldip Singh's statement became grist in the *Khalistani* propaganda mill. One prominent NRI *Khalistan* ideologue circulated copies of the news reports through the Internet with the following comments:

> When the Indian Supreme Court describes our situation as 'worse than genocide' why are Akali leaders so shy to espouse Khalistan? We are being killed and cremated just like the Jews in Nazi Germany. The Jewish people knew that the only way to prevent their complete annihilation was to establish a sovereign homeland of their own. The Sikh Nation's situation is no less dire...

This statement, with the authority of a Supreme Court judge behind it, has been repeated in numerous international fora as evidence of India's 'poor human rights record'. No subsequent judgement by any court will ever entirely undo the harm this single sweeping observation has already done.

The problem, however, is not restricted to the potential for error and injustice in individual cases. Judges today perceive themselves as the unaccountable defenders of a unarticulated 'philosophy', the contents of which they alone appear to be aware of. The result, as it manifests itself piecemeal in conflicting and contradictory judgements and orders, is total jurisprudential disarray. Seervai expresses this differently, but is no less damning in his evaluation:

> The most important cause of prevailing uncertainty in the law is that a number of Supreme Court Judges firmly believe that a certain 'philosophy' and certain 'values', inhere in our Constitution, and it is their duty to give effect to that 'philosophy' and those 'values'. Since the 'philosophy' and the 'values' are not formulated, they cannot be subjected to judicial or professional criticism...[18]

This belief, he continues, "is responsible for the judicial indiscipline which is responsible for the disconcerting unpredictability of Supreme Court judgements."[19] This unpredictability, he argues further, "is largely due to the fact that several Judges ask themselves the wrong question: "This is how I wish to decide, what shall I say?", instead of asking themselves the right question: "What is the law?" This attitude has resulted in...fatally flawed... judgements.[20]

These 'fatally flawed judgements' have catastrophic effects as they echo through the subordinate judiciary. The Supreme Court lays down the law for all the High Courts and lower courts throughout the country. Any conflict, inconsistency, ambiguity or confusion in any of its judgements multiplies itself a hundred-fold in the High Courts, and many thousand-fold in lower courts, as lawyers and litigants discover new loopholes and opportunities for, if nothing else, protracting the processes of litigation. It is significant, in this regard, to note that judicial delay almost always benefits the wrongdoer. If the Supreme Court sincerely seeks to identify the causes for the unmanageable problem of mounting pendencies, it will discover perhaps the most important one in the confusion of philosophies and directives emanating from its own portals.

These, then, are the conditions prevailing in the Supreme Court. Regarding the subordinate judiciary, the less said, the better. It is sufficient to note, for example, that the conviction rate in criminal cases as it stands today is below six-and-a-half per cent. The processes that result in these rare convictions, moreover, are so erratic and arbitrary that the results are more lottery than law. The fact of the matter is that an overwhelming majority of criminals are going free. In any event, it is my belief that anything that an injured party may secure at the end of a process of litigation that could extend across several decades cannot deserve the title 'justice'.

Despite all these failings, it is indeed amazing that we are, in the Indian judiciary, confronted with an institution that has placed itself beyond the scope of accountability to any other authority. And it has accomplished this by its own fiat in that 'fatally flawed decision'—the *Second Judges' Transfer Case.* India is the only country in the world where judges select themselves; where they determine their own transfers; and where they discipline—or decline to discipline—themselves. There are no declared norms for these processes, and no accountability once these processes are complete. No public or executive scrutiny is countenanced, and a handful of judges exercise all this authority by themselves in accordance to norms, 'values' and 'philosophies' that are [presumably] known only to this privileged fraternity.

In recent years a curious proposition has, nevertheless, increasingly been articulated: that judges are 'accountable' to the 'people'. No effort is made to clarify what 'accountability' and 'the people' actually mean in this context. Were judges politicians, of course, there would be little difficulty in understanding these terms. They would confront the electorate periodically, and would [at least theoretically] be called to account for their activities in the preceding period. The judiciary, thankfully, is not required to compromise its dignity through any such ritual. Nonetheless, we are constantly reminded—especially in the context of judicial activism and the flood of public interest litigation that occupies so much of the Court's time today—that the judiciary 'enjoys popular support' since people are 'disgusted with politicians and bureaucrats', as though the judiciary is a party in the contest for political power [which, at the present time in history, I believe it is]. At a purely visceral level, these arguments are accepted by the less informed both in the public and among those who propound them. They are based, however, on a gross misunderstanding of the position of the judiciary within the democratic framework.

The judiciary is, no doubt, an institution integral to democratic governance; it is not, however, a democratic institution. The noted American jurist, Professor Schwartz, in fact states that it is, in the context of its power of judicial review, "basically an undemocratic institution. Through the exercise of its review power the Supreme Court may enable the will even of the great majority of the people to be frustrated."[21] Irving Kristol expresses as somewhat differently: "The Supreme Court is not—and was never supposed to be—a democratic institution; it is a republican institution which counterbalances the activities of our various democratic institutions."[22]

Constitutional doctrine, it has been remarked, "ought to be, as nearly as possible, a steady line on the graph of history, always upward, avoiding peaks and valleys.[23] The jurisprudential turmoil that we are currently witnessing is, to my mind, not a sign of sagacity or statesmanship, but a sign of desperation in a system on the verge of collapse. Three criteria have been defined for the identification of a system of justice on its last legs:

1. That people come to believe that inefficiency and delay will drain even a just judgement of its value.
2. That people who have long been exploited in the smaller transactions of daily life come to believe that courts cannot vindicate their legal rights from fraud and over-reaching.
3. That people come to believe the Law—in the larger sense—cannot fulfil its primary function to protect them and their families in their home, at their work, and on the public streets.[24]

These circumstances manifestly prevail in India today.

I believe it is when institutions and individuals are failing to fulfil their own true functions and obligations that their appetite for power and aggrandisement is the greatest. I believe that this, ultimately, is the character of the adventure on which the Indian judiciary is presently engaged.

If these unfortunate and unconstitutional trends are to be checked, it is essential to set up an independent Judicial Commission which would be responsible, not only for appointments and transfers, but also to see to it that judges perform their duties in keeping with the high traditions of the legal profession and the Judiciary, and for the investigation of, and prosecution on, charges of corruption and judicial misconduct. Such a body should also be required by statute to publish an Annual State of Justice Report, with a complete categorywise Statistical Break-up of cases, pendencies and disposals; as well as a comprehensive summary of the main jurisprudential trends emerging from critical judgements. The latter would go some distance towards ensuring that, even where individual decisions apply contrary or contradictory principles, the approved jurisprudential position of the Supreme Court—and its consistency with constitutional provisions—is unambiguous.

No Commission comprised people drawn from the area or the fraternity that requires reform will ever be able to bring about the requisite reforms. The proposed Judicial Commission must be widely representative—with those who have been subjected to the tyranny and the caprice of the judicial system given a prominent voice.

REFERENCES

1. Carroll, Lewis, *The Annotated Alice: Through The Looking Glass,* Penguin Books, 1978, p. 269.
2. Venkatachaliah, Justice M. N., 'Role of Judiciary in Good Government', Ninth D. R. Mankekar Memorial Lecture, India International Centre, October 11, 1997.
3. Anand, Justice A. S., P. Babulu Reddy Foundation Lecture on "Victims of Crime: Unseen Side", reported in *The Times of India,* September 30, 1997.
4. By virtue of the Supreme Court's majority judgement in what is known as the *Second Judges' Transfer Case [Supreme Court Advocates Assn. on Record v. Union,* ('94) A.SC. 268, (1993) 4 SSC 441]. The decision itself is regarded as unconstitutional by constitutional experts. Cf. H. M. Seervai, *Constitutional Law of India,* Fourth Edition, Volume 3, N. Tripathi Pvt. Ltd., 1996, "The Second Judges' Case— A Fatally Flawed Decision", pp. 2928-70.

5. Seervai, H. M., *Constitutional Law of India,* Fourth Edition, Volume 3, N. Tripathi Pvt. Ltd., 1996, p. 2927.
6. *Ibid.,* pp. 2927-28.
7. Cited in Seervai, *Ibid.,* p. 2967.
8. Gupta, Anupam, speech at the meeting for the Bar Association in honour of the visiting Chief Justice of India, Justice M.N. Venkatachaliah on August 28, 1993, in the High Court premises.
9. Anonymous, cited in Judge Harold J. Rothwax, *Guilty: The Collapse of Criminal Justice,* Random House, New York, 1996, p. 186.
10. Mahajan, Krishan, "Can a HC judge with 'criminal case' be confirmed?" *Indian Express,* September 8, 1997.
11. *Supreme Court Advocates Assn. on Record v. Union,* ('94) A.SC. 268, (1993) 4 SCC 443.
12. *Op. cit.,* p. 2928.
13, *Ibid.,* p. 2881.
14. *Jones v. National Coal Board* (1957) 2QB 55 at p. 64 and citing Bacon's "Essay of Council Civil and Moral", *of Judicature.*
15. *Op. cit.,* pp. 2868-69.
16. *Ibid.,* p. 2871.
17. *The Indian Express,* July 24, 1996.
18. *Op. cit.,* p. 2885.
19. *Ibid.*
20. *Ibid.,* p. 2965.
21. Cited in *Ibid.,* p. 2892.
22. Kristol, Irving, *Reflections of a Neoconservative: Looking Back, Looking Ahead,* Allied Publishers Pvt. Ltd., 1986, p. 93. The remarks are in the context of the American Constitution, but they apply equally to the Indian.
23. Burger, Judge Warren E., *Delivery of Justice,* The College of William and Mary Press & West Publishing Co., 1990, p. 24.
24. *Ibid.,* p. 44.

18

ASSESSING THE JUDICIARY

Joginder Singh

The Constitution of India has created three separate wings of the Government. The job of the executive is to govern as per the laws passed by the Legislature. The judiciary judges whether the game of laws enforcement is being played fairly. Article 14 of the constitution guarantees equality to all citizens. It also includes equality in the enforcement of laws irrespective of the status of the persons concerned. While the constitution endeavours to provide equality to all citizens, the entire societal structure is based on inequality. A poor man cannot afford the best legal talent to get him the justice. Due to the huge population, there is naturally huge litigation and the pendency of the cases in the courts of the country is over 3 crores. Even if no new cases are instituted, it will take at least 10 years to clear the backlog of the cases. So by a conservative estimate, if there is total peace and tranquillity, that much time is required to liquidate what is pending. It is, not possible to expect any such utopian situation. The justice should not only be done, but should also appear to be done. Whatever a witness says has to be reduced to writing. In the interest of justice and fairplay, the accused has to be given a chance to question and cross question the witness. Speaking is one thing but writing is another. The time taken in writing is more than double. Then it has to be sifted and only relevant evidence has to be used.

We naturally become impatient when we find that a case takes ages to be disposed of. However prompt and efficient a judge may be, he cannot humanly dispose of more than one case per working day. This will also depend on whether all the witnesses have turned up. By a very generous estimate, it will come to about 20 to 22 cases per month. But the institution of cases is far higher in the Courts. *The Tribune* dated August 17, 1997 carried the following report under the heading Random thoughts "Delhi Police Commissioner told this correspondent that 80000 police cases or challans were pending in the city courts. If 100 cases were settled in a year—an impossible task—it would take 800 years for the citizen to obtain justice. To add to this horrifying prospect, it is stated that the police, working from the early hours of morning till late in the evening, has no time to attend to small culpable crimes such as vandalism in a home by a crime prone man, misuse of office by an area security committee member, pilferage and breach of trust, repeatedly brought to the notice of the police officers. Crime thrives with punishment way behind. Not surprisingly the police has no credibility; it is neither feared nor respected by the people. It is the sheer pressure of numbers which is responsible for backlog in every sector in our lives, whether it be the schools or colleges, or hospitals, or municipal and civic services. The sheer numbers itself force people to jump the queue and get their work done, through legal means, if possible and through not so legal means if every other mean fails. We, as a Nation are responsible for the malady. Those who can afford see their way either through the influence or money".

The result is that it is the common man who suffers. Yes, there is a way out. But it does not lie through criticism or apportioning blame or showing who is one up. It lies through the route of conciliation and every part of the governing system working in unison and harmony to achieve a set of goals. The way we go about litigating right up to the highest Court will in way is going to improve the situation. One more factor is that it is not easy to criticise the judicial officer, however just the criticism may be, in the view of the person criticising, without attracting the apprehension of contempt of court proceedings. The border line between the contempt and criticism is very thin. Crossing is and can be dangerous for the person attempting it. In the case of contempt of Court proceedings, the judge is both a judge and a prosecutor. Recently, Rajasthan High Court has held that all criticism cannot be contempt. Unless the Supreme Court hands down a final decision, the ambiguity is likely to continue. It is the basic law that a judge should not be a prosecutor. Perhaps, it will be a good idea if the contempt proceedings initiated by one judicial officer are tried by the next higher judicial officer. A number of complaints about some Courts and the staff connected with the Court are common. Even the CBI registered a case against an official connected with the High Court on the complaint of the Court itself a few months back. By convention or practice or instructions, all complaints against the judicial officers are referred to the High Court or Supreme Court.

It is heartening to note that the High Courts and the Supreme Court have descended very harshly against some judicial officers. Quite a few of them have been dismissed. But the fact remains, much more can be done and should be done in judicial system as in Executive. While levelling charges, the efforts should be to improve and not destroy the system. I am sure, even the Judiciary would welcome any just criticism and suggestions for causing improvements. However, the only problem arises that a layman who is not familiar with the legal niceties, may unwittingly commit contempt, while criticising the judiciary. The legal system has a serious loophole that the person concerned who knows best about his case cannot argue it unless he holds a law degree. Law is nothing, but a codified common sense. A beginning can be made that should a person want to explain or argue his own case, he should have the full freedom to do. He can be made to give an undertaking that he is doing so at his own risk and he would not ask to be represented by a lawyer later. This will ensure that he does his homework thoroughly and if he loses by lack of knowledge of law, he cannot blame anybody else.

Whatever be lapses of legal system, it is important to bear in mind whether the judiciary has all the infrastructure to handle the workload it is required to handle. There is a limit for every institution to handle the work it is required to do. If it is not given all the wherewithal, it will naturally not be able to dispose of the work assigned to it. It is essential to study its requirements, manpower-wise, equipmentwise and the basic facilities it requires for functioning. In many places, the courts are functioning from buildings which should have been demolished long ago or at least properly repaired and whitewashed. A judge, unlike an ordinary bureaucrat is not expected to chase his requirements. The result is for all to see. There are overcrowded and overworked Courts. For instance in 1994 a total of 55.1 lakhs cases under the Indian Penal Code were registered as against 60.1 lakh cases in 1995. But in 1994 a backlog of 4759521 cases were pending for trial. Out of this figure only 736797 cases were taken up for trial. It can be presumed very safely that only a few cases would be of 1994 and the rest would be the backlog.

As against 60.1 lakh IPC cases, in 1995, only 5042744 were sent up or pending for trial. Out of this only 763944 were tried. In 1994, trial was completed only in 15.5 per cent cases sent up for trial and in 1995, it was 15.1 per cent. So by a very generous estimate, there is a built-in delay of nearly six years in the disposal of the IPC cases by the Courts. If a case is registered in 1997, the reasonable hope for its completion cannot be earlier than after seven years. A judicial officer is also a human being. He can also fall sick, have family commitments and personal problems. He will also need to proceed on leave. While judiciary may not have been able to dispose of all the cases filed before it in a given year, it is pertinent to question whether the country has given it all the wherewithal to dispose of all the work assigned to it in a reasonable frame of time.

With the workload which judiciary is facing, one solution seems to be to simplify all the laws. There should be more and more of compounding of cases. We should become a conciliatory society rather than a litigant one. There is need to simplify the judicial procedures to reduce the unnecessary workload of the Courts particularly for admission of appeal. Even where a case has been decided, by the Highest Court in the country, some people go on agitating till their point of view is conceded. There is a happy situation, no doubt, because in many cases the Apex Court and Constitutional Courts have refused to interfere.

Still sometimes, people with a lot of money power go right up to the Highest Court for simple matters like the bail or change of venue of trial. Happily the judiciary has acted correctly within the framework of law. So when those who wish to judge the judiciary should ask the "Physician, first heal thy self."

19

INDIAN JUDICIARY: SOME PERSONAL ENCOUNTERS

R.K. Takkar

During my 35 years in the Indian Administrative Service, I have had varied and interesting encounters with the judiciary and the judges.

My first exposure to the judicial system was attachment to a subordinate magistrate at Saharanpur in the second year of my service. As a part of my field training I was to sit with a number of magistrates while they were conducting trials. I must confess that the exposure left me shocked. It would have shocked any young man who was uninitiated about the ways the judiciary and had had only a theoretical image of how judicial system operates. While the magistrate was hearing arguments from two opposing valuable lawyers in the centre of the court room, two of the court clerks were separately examining witnesses in two opposite corners of the court room. It was meant to be an open public court and it was so. The number of people coming in and going out was totally uncontrolled and would have been perhaps unmanageable. The court room resembled more like a railway platform than a place where the sacred duty of dispensation of public justice was being performed.

I honestly and fondly believed that this magistrate, would be an exception to the rule, but I was sorely disappointed when call of my training took me to the court of other subordinate magistrates. The only marginal difference came to my notice in the court of Addl. District Magistrate (Judicial) who was the District head of the subordinate judicial magistracy. I sat through a famous trial in this court. A senior ICS officer of Punjab Cadre, Shri R.P. Kapoor, was facing trial in his court in a case, which had been transferred at his request from courts of Punjab to the court at Saharanpur on his contention that since the then Chief Minister of Punjab was taking improper interest in his case, he was not likely to get a fair trial in any court in Punjab. The case was widely reported in the newspapers and I went through the sensation, in the very second year of my service of being part of history in the making. However the trial left a bad taste in my mouth because one day I found Shri Kapoor almost begging some of the senior magistrates for authenticating a document that was to be produced before the court. The Presiding Officer was obviously not approached because the document had to be filed with him. I was yet to be vested with magisterial powers. Therefore, my authentication had no legal authority. Two other magistrates who had come to watch the proceedings and were sitting on the side of the Presiding Officer, somehow strangely and till now for reasons difficult for me to understand, shook their heads when Shri Kapoor approached them for attesting the document. Humiliation and helplessness was writ large on the face of this distinguished and senior civil servant.

My most hilarious experience of the judiciary during this period of training came to me when I was attached to the District and Sessions Judge for three sessions trials as a part of my training and confirmation in service. The requirement was that an IAS probationer records the evidence along with the court and writes a parallel judgement in each case in strict confidence which are evaluated by the Presiding Officer for determining the suitability of the probationer to continue in service. I performed the task very earnestly and put in a lot of hard work, but to my horror, I found that in all the three cases, verdict by the District and Sessions Judge was different from mine. I thought it was the end of my career which was yet to begin. However, my colleagues subordinate magistracy who had travelled on this road earlier assured me that there was nothing to fear and that what was crucial was not the final decision, but the quality of recording of evidence and the appraisal of evidence as such. Either this must have been true or the District and Sessions

Judge must have been a very generous soul, because my career did proceed uninterrupted. Sometimes I wonder I might have been right.

In due course I was conferred powers of Third Class, Second Class and First Class Magistrates after intervals of 3 to 6 months. This provided me an opportunity to try petty cases under the Cr. P.C. as well as I.P.C. and a body of law loosely described as Miscellaneous Acts. This period was also treated as a part of an IAS Officer's training on the job. Strangely, the two court orderlies were of great help in promoting my career because of the help they rendered in conducting my work as a court. Although totally unlettered, they were fully clued up on the court procedures and were also familiar with provisions of major laws. They could easily identify the law books which were part of the reference material for day-to-day conduct of proceedings. What was most intriguing to me at that point of time and continues to be so till now, was the assistance they used to render in framing the chargesheet against an accused. The moment either would discover that their Magistrate was omitting to include a particular section of IPC or a Misc. Law, he would come quietly to my side and whisper in my ear the particular section and withdraw equally quietly. Of course, the advocates on both the sides knew what was happening.

My first judgement as a Magistrate proved disturbing for my personal life. No doubt, it was a milestone in my professional career and personal growth, but it robbed me of my peace of mind for quite some time. It was a case of simple hurt, I found the accused guilty and gave them a maximum punishment of 6 months' simple imprisonment. I had spent a lot of time on absorbing every little piece of evidence on the file and critically examining it before I came to the conclusion that they were guilty, but still I was attacked by the fear that I may be wrong. Similarly, I was not sure whether I was right in having inflicted the maximum punishment permissible under the law. I shared my doubts with my magistrate friends in the lunch room. They had obviously no judgement to pass on whether the accused were guilty or not, but were unanimous that the award of 6 months' imprisonment was excessive, ordinarily the maximum prescribed punishment should be awarded in cases where there were extranuating circumstances. The accused had a right to appeal. They kept coming to my court to collect copies of various papers which they needed for filing the appeal. Sometime I would run into them in the premises of the Collectorate. A strange thing happened. In stead of their trying to escape my attention, I got into the habit of not looking them into their eyes straight. The strange behaviour on my part reached a climax when one day my wife and I; (we were newly married) were going in a rickshaw in the bazzar when I found these three accused walking from the opposite side. They hardly noticed me, but I directed the rickshawala into a wrong lane without explaining the reason to my wife who kept wondering what had happened.

The District Magistrate of Saharanpur, who was responsible for my proper training, was very keen that I must do two things during my district training. One, to record a dying declaration and the other to witness a hanging. Both were memorable experiences. The dying declaration was recorded in a hospital in the presence of a doctor when the patient was finding it hardly possible to speak and was almost inarticulate. He was coughing and vomitting very badly and had to be attended to by the doctor after every sentence or two. It almost took two hours of recording a statement almost half a page or so. The paper contained more evidence of his vomit than his thoughts at the time of his wordly exit. The second experience left me very disturbed and I went without meals that day. A young man who had murdered his wife because of infidelity, was being hanged. I had accompanied a senior Magistrate and the Civil Surgeon to the Central Jail for witnessing the hanging very early morning. Before he was taken to the hangman's noose, he hugged the Jail Supdt. and touched his feet and asked for his forgiveness. The Jail Supdt. later told us that this kind of behaviour on the part of a condemned prisoner was typical because during this period they come to be attached to any person who shows even the smallest favour or affection. His relatives had been waiting outside the jail to collect his body, but he had instructed the jail staff that it should not be given to any of his relations. They went back disappointed, but all of them were in tears. The actual hanging was much less dramatic than what I had thought. It took a split of a second and the body was brought down for examination by the Civil Surgeon who declared the man dead. The senior Magistrate, the Civil Surgeon and the Jail Supdt. signed some of the documents and all was over and so was a part of my training.

It was during the period I joined the IAS that the movement for separation of judicial from executive had gathered force and laws were being passed in different parts of the country for carrying through the separation. Therefore, after my training I had no opportunity really to conduct the proceedings of a criminal court, but I have had long experience of a revenue court. Learning from Saharanpur experience of how subordinate magistrates brought disgrace to themselves and the judicial system, I became a keen votary of strict decorum and discipline in the court. I never allowed more than one case to be conducted in my court at one time. I was one of the few officers who wrote all their judgements themselves and did not depend on the readers and other court staff for assistance in this matter. I tried one simple reform in procedure which helped in speeding up the disposal of the cases. At the time of admission of an appeal I would not summon the respondents. It served one of the three purposes all of which helped in early disposal of the cases. Firstly, it would dishearten such appellants whose only purpose would be to drag on the litigation and cause embarrassment, irritation and expenses to the other party. Secondly, it enabled me in many cases to actually dispose of the appeal without summoning the opposite party. It may be mentioned that hearing the other party is not necessary if the order proposed to be passed is not adverse to them. Thirdly, the respondents would appear on their own wondering what had happened and that things may not go against them. This would save lot of time in issuing of summons and the mischief and corruption that goes in serving or not serving the summons from a court.

During my long innings in Government service in senior positions, I could not have escaped contempt notices from High Courts. There were plenty of them, but all excepting one was directed at me as Head of the organisation for decisions of my subordinates. In fact, this part of the judicial system did cause irritation and wasteful expenditure of time. I find little justification for a practice where a Secretary to Government of India is hauled up for contempt arising out of the act of his subordinates. I am no expert of law. I have the highest regard for the judiciary. But I am not sure whether the law really requires such a procedure in every case. This practice needs to be reviewed by law experts in order to save a lot of higher management time. I am confident this can be done without compromising the popular respect for the judiciary and speedy endorcement of its decisions.

The only time I was hauled up for personal contempt by the High Court of J&K was a case in which the Government had appointed me as an Enquiry Officer into a disciplinary proceedings against a doctor. I had proceeded with the enquiry whereas the doctor contended that the Government order did not carry out the wishes of the court correctly in an interim order. In the contempt proceedings filed by him before the court, I was asked to appear personally. However, the Hon'ble Judge was very kind, I sat amongst the Advocates and the visitors and was not made to stand in the box earmarked for the accused. To my great relief the contempt petition was dismissed on the same day and I proceeded with the enquiry.

I have no pretention of adding to the voluminous literature on judicial reforms, but I would like to suggest two small things which could possibly help—firstly, the subordinate court rarely use the provision of law under which a complainant who comes up with a false and mischievous complaint can be prosecuted. Incidence of such complaints is very high. They are filed so as to settle personal scores and exert pressure in the settlement of civil disputes. Besides causing considerable inconvenience to thousands of citizens they waste the precious times of courts who have more important matters to handle. Most of the courts who let go such complainants are indulgent on the consideration that procecuting them will add to the court work. They need to consider the long-term effect of taking notice of such complaints and sending a few complainants to jail. This will not only bring relief to the citizens but also result in less work for the courts. Secondly, I have been intrigued over the years by the time the High Courts and even the Supreme Court are required under our judicial system to spend on petty personal matters of private citizens. There is a famous case of two business tycoons brothers fighting over the ownership of a Mercedes car which came to be agitated in one High Court and ended up in the Supreme Court. The Supreme Court and the High Courts were designed for matters of higher priority to the citizens and the nation and it appears that somewhere either in the making of the Constitution or law or its interpretation, the system has suffered a distortion.

A lot has been said and written about the long and large pendency before the courts of law in the country. A number of solutions have been offered. Benefitting from my experience at the receiving end, I feel the senior public servants can help a lot in the disposal of the cases before the courts. Firstly, they can help in creating less cases for the courts in service matters. It is reported that almost 3/4th of the cases in some High Courts relate to service matters of public servants. The senior civil servants can help in the timely formulation of service rules and their just and fair enforcement. My experience tells me that senior civil servants spend very little time in understanding the service rules applicable to others and in their just application. Secondly, senior public servants can help if they were to spend time on the petitions by aggrieved citizens in an effort to understand whether the petition has a merit and whether the matter can be settled by not contesting the case or entering into an out of court settlement. On the other hand, the response is generally routine and pedestrian.

One common response is to contest the case since a decision by a Government authority is under challenge. Little thought is given to the conduct of the authority, the character of that decision, and the injustice done to a private citizen. Some timid souls even when they realise that the prayer made in the petition should be accepted, choose to contest lest in the current vitiated environment of public distrust in the honesty of the civil servants their conduct becomes suspect. Another routine response is to get busy with the logistics of defending the case, i.e. engaging a lawyer, preparing of reply, etc. and no thought being given as such to the question of whether the case should be contested at all. The concept and principle of 'sub-judice' is very helpful to such civil servants because they justify their lack of action or courage in the name of the matter pending with the court. One could go to the extent of saying that the principle of 'sub-judice' gets a lot of credit which belongs to cowardice or lack of public concern.

20

REFORMING THE JUDICIARY

N.K. Singh

Apart from increasing criminalisation of politics and growing corruption at high places, it is the failure of our legal system to deal with this twin-problems which has been causing serious concern. Criminal justice system has failed to produce "desired results", this is what former Chief Justice of India, Mr. M.N. Venkatachaliah, observed quite a few years ago. Prior to that on November 26, 1985, the then Chief Justice, Mr. P.N. Bhagwati, had stated at the Law Day address that "I am pained to observe that judicial system is almost on the verge of collapse; these are very strong words I am using, but it is with considerable anguish that I say so."

Two main limbs of criminal justice system are, the police including the enforcement agency like the CBI and the judiciary. The blame for the sorry state of affairs has to be taken by both. But while the police and the CBI have been everybody's favourite 'weeping boys' not much is said about the judiciary which has also failed us. I saw this and felt it as much during my long inning in the CBI.

I recall what was known as 'Kissa Kursi Kaa' case. The film 'Kissa Kursi Kaa' was a satire on the ways of Mrs. Gandhi and her alleged corrupt practices, particularly centering round her son, late Sanjay Gandhi. When the producer, Amrith Mehta, was struggling to get certificate for exhibition, emergency was clamped over the country and all the film materials of Mehta was confiscated under the Defence of India rules. During the hearing of his petition, the Supreme Court Bench, headed by the Chief Justice, wanted to see the film. It is at this stage that according to the CBI case, a criminal conspiracy was hatched to prevent the Supreme Court from seeing the film, a false affidavit was filed saying that the film materials were missing, when in fact all the materials of the film were brought from Bombay to Delhi in newly purchased 13 trunks, taken to Maruti factory and burnt there. The Special Judge after a lengthy trial convicted V.C. Shukla and late Sanjay Gandhi and sentenced them to two years rigorous imprisonment along with fines. When the case was being heard in an appeal by the Supreme Court under the Special Court Act of 1979, following general elections, the Government changed at the Centre and Mrs. Gandhi became Prime Minister. The new Government replaced the Special Public Prosecutor, Shri Ram Jethmalani with Mr. J.S. Wasu. The hearing of the appeal started on 26 November 1979, with arguments on behalf of Sanjay Gandhi and V.C. Shukla. They concluded their arguments towards last week of February, 1980. When the turn of Special Counsel for argument on behalf of CBI came, Mr. Wasu concluded it within 15 minutes. The PTI reported that "Mr. Wasu, who folded up his arguments within 15 minutes, in reply to the arguments advanced by Mr. Rajinder Singh, Counsel for Mr. V.C. Shukla and Mr. K.L. Arora, Counsel for Mr. Sanjay Gandhi over the last three months, told the Court that he had nothing more than what was already on Court's record to substantiate his case." "We could not overlaborate the points already made by the prosecution in the trial court." Mr. Justice Kaushal put a specific query. Could he answer the defence arguments about Mr. Sanjay Gandhi's absence during the dates on which burning of the film was said to have taken place? "Will you elaborate the point?" The judges asked. Mr. Wasu boldly replied, "The burning of the film is not supported by any evidence" (*The Statesman* dated 22 Feb. 1980). When Mr. Wasu sat down, the Court reserved judgement. Distinguished journalist and an eminent legal commentator, Mr. A.G. Noorani, wrote in the 'Opinion' (Weekly Copy No. 5) that a worn out jest in Hyderabad Courts was a lawyer telling the Court, "The law is best known to your Lordship and the facts are on the record, my arguments are over." Ultimately, the Supreme Court set aside the order of conviction of the Special Judge and acquitted Mr. V.C. Shukla and late Sanjay Gandhi of the charges. Commenting on the case, eminent jurist and Member of Parliament, who had conducted the case on behalf of the state in the Sessions Court Mr. Ram Jethmalani said in a statement to *Decan Herald,* "From my knowledge of the case I can say that vital evidence was neither noticed by the Judges on their own nor pointed out by the counsel for the State. Every criticism of the evidence by the accused had a fair explanation which required judicial consideration. The Judges have shut their eyes to light when light was available in plenty. A terrible blow has been dealt to the dignity of the Supreme Court, consequent of which will be tragic in the extreme."

During the hearing of the case on January 29, I was forced to leave my official residence at Chanakya Puri, New Delhi, and taken to city police station, Gurgaon, by Bhajan Lal police in a false case. They had come to my residence in the early hours of the morning when it was still dark and the purpose was obviously sinister. During the hearing of the appeal, when the Supreme Court reopened after Christmas vacation, I sought leave to intervene through my counsel, Mr. V.M. Tarkunde. The intervention, Mr. Tarkunde argued, had become necessary as after the change of Government, the accused had merged with the State. I was some times at the receiving end of some of the adverse observations made by the Judges. I had particularly felt hurt when the Judges repeatedly referred to me as 'this fellow'. While hearing the writ petition of Amrith Mehta, the Bench presided over by the Chief Justice himself had repeatedly asked for screening of the film, 'Kissa Kursi Kaa'. This was thwarted by the accused with the impunity and the court was fed with down-right falsehood that the film was not traceable. This was one reason why I had worked ceaselessly for the detection and prosecution of the accused. As a public servant who had discharged a very sensitive and difficult assignment, I thought I was entitled to better treatment irrespective of judgement on the merit of the case. My intervention petition through Mr. Tarkunde was disposed of by the Judges saying that they did not intend to make any remarks against me in their judgement and that in case they did, they would call upon Mr. Tarkunde to argue the matter. In view of this, Mr. Tarkunde did not get chance to argue the case which should have exposed the manner in which the Government counsel Mr. Wasu folded the arguments on behalf of the Government within 15 minutes.

Almost a decade later came another sensational case, namely St. Kitts case, allegedly involving highest political functionaries. Godman Chandraswami was under investigation as chief architect for executing the conspiracy to fabricate certain bank accounts in St. Kitts in the name of Ajay Singh, son of V.P. Singh, with the latter shown as beneficiary. Chandraswami had made himself scarce after V.P. Singh took over as Prime Minister. He decided to return to the country 15 days after Chandrashekar took over as Prime Minister in November, 1990. Chandraswami succeeded in getting interim anticipatory bail on 23 November, 1990, even before he landed in the country. Under my instructions, the CBI opposed grant of anticipatory bail to him when the matter came up for regular hearing. Chandraswami, however, succeeded in getting anticipatory bail. It can be stated with respect that we have always felt that courts have been rather liberal in granting anticipatory bails to notorious criminals whose activities have global ramifications. Grant of anticipatory bail to Chandraswami in St. Kitts case was one such instance. The High Court, however, imposed certain conditions which included that he would make himself available to CBI for examination. Basking under the patronage of the then Prime Minister, Chandrashekar and the Law Minister, Subramaniam Swamy, Chandraswami completely disregarded repeated attempts by CBI to get him for examination. In the meantime, he obtained permission from Delhi High Court in another case (Lakubai Pathak case) to leave India. We moved the Delhi High Court the very next day through a petition for restraining Chandraswami from going out of India. Our request, however, was turned down by the High Court, although the court gave a firm date to Chandraswami to appear before the CBI for his examination.

During this intervening period between the order of Delhi High Court and the date of his appearance I was abruptly transferred out of CBI. I felt enough was enough, and decided to fight a legal battle against this malafide transfer with a design to subvert the investigation. I filed a petition before the Central

Administrative Tribunal. It was heard on Ist April, 1991. The Tribunal not only dismissed the petition but made an observation saying that "It was the responsibility of the Government to decide whether a case which has been taken up for investigation should be processed or how it has to be processed." This is in the realm of execution policy, which has to be decided by the Minister concerned and not by the civil servants working under him. The civil servant, however, highly placed, is bound to implement the policy decision and directions given by the Minister concerned. In other words, the Tribunal held that the Minister had the right to interfere in the investigation of a criminal case and a civil servant was bound to implement whatever instructions were issued in the course of investigation. I went in appeal to the Supreme Court against the judgement. We contended that this doctrine set out by the Tribunal was subversive of the rule of law and made the entire criminal law an instrument to be used by the politicians in power according to their will or for self-interest. The Supreme Court not only dismissed my petition against malafide transfer but also ignored this pernicious doctrine of the CAT. The highest court, it may be stated with respect, failed to protect an enforcement officer who had earned the wrath of the executive only because he wanted to pursue investigation in a case involving highest political functionaries vigorously. In fact, while appearing on my behalf, the eminent lawyer Mr. Ram Jethmalani had urged the court to find out why the investigation into the St. Kitts case which had reached crucial stage in March, 1991, was still pending investigation. We failed on this count also. It was only when a public interest petition was filed a few years later that the Supreme Court intervened in the matter and as a result chargesheet was filed in St. Kitts case, but by the time enough damage had been done to the case and much of the valuable evidence had been lost.

Another glaring case that comes to mind is one of 'Bofors' in which once the Delhi High Court quashed even the FIR filed by CBI resulting into delay in getting the banks papers from Swiss Banks.

The recent judicial activism, however, has come as a welcome relief. This has rekindled the people's confidence and faith in our criminal justice system. But this is only a shortterm measure. Some longterm measures are required to streamline the investigating agency like CBI and insulate it from corrupt political interference. It is necessary that an effective and transparent agency like 'Lokpal' be instituted at the earliest. There is a need to bring about electoral and legal reforms to prevent corrupt politicians from getting into the Parliament and Legislatures and seats of power. Unless we do this, the ruie of law and for that matter the parliamentary democracy will not be safe in the country.

21

JUDICIAL ACTIVISM—NEW DIMENSIONS OF POLICE ACCOUNTABILITY

H.S. Sandhu

The public perception of police services in our country has become that of a corrupt, incompetent and insensitive administrative monoliths which would rather play safe than take courageous decisions. Unfortunately, in these and other allegations levelled against the police, the impression has grown that police leadership has failed with the task of controlling its members, so it cannot be trusted with the discipline of its members and therefore, the support to have some form of external checks upon the organisation has also escalated.

So, the issue of police accountability is alive once again! The daily experiences of most people in India, leave little doubt that the police action leaves much to be desired. The need to make members of the 'police force' feel responsible about their actions and the existence of some agency that could demand its accountability has become a burning issue.

The expression 'police accountability' is certainly extremely relevant in today's context when many set practices are being re-examined and revalued, many apparently settled administrative norms are being adjusted and redefined. In simple and practical terms, it is the question of answerability of the police to the popularly elected government in a democracy, or, further generalising it, to the elected representatives of the people. In a still wider sense, the accountability of the police in a democracy, which idealistically speaking, stands for a government of the people, by the people and for the people is to every member of the society whom the profession professes to serve.

Indeed the concept of accountability to the members of the public at large is particularly significant for the police whose activities cover, rather impinge upon, many facets of individual's life and his relationship with others. And to that extent, it provides the police both a test and an opportunity to prove their bonafides, their worth and their utility. The fact that the propriety of police action and behaviour has in recent times come into serious question, indeed makes the issue fit for a lively discussion.

An obvious question arises. How then is this accountability of the police determined and worked out on the ground? Three spheres of accountability have been spelt out by various commissions and conferences: the police are accountable to the people, the police have an accountability to the law and the police functionaries are accountable to the organisation.

From the point of view of the police, the question is what role the law of the land lays down for them; or, in other words, what is the precise constitutional position of the police in our federal type of democracy? The point to be determined for the police is the degree of what we call functional independence. How much should the police of today be insulated against any outside interference to enable them to discharge their duties and responsibilities without any fear or favour? Viewed from the other side, it is also of considerable importance that all public services in a democracy are ultimately accountable to the elected representatives of the people. Interestingly, in this unequivocal call for making police accountable to the people's representatives, the law makers have conveniently forgotten that police is accountable in law to courts, to superior officers and through the department to the minister in charge of the Home portfolio. The police is always accountable to the citizens for without their cooperation it virtually cannot function.

The police, easily one of the major public services in the country, will, therefore, have to be guided and moulded by what role is thought appropriate of them in a democratic set-up. The moot point in the life of a nation is—how much of a citizen's life should be controlled or rather overviewed by the police.

Nowhere any precise definition of the constitutional role of the police is found in any of the statute books. The only statutory definition of the role of the police is available in the Police Act of 1861 vintage, which by virtue of the sanctity attached to it should by now be called the police 'Bible' of the country. Whatever be the reasons or circumstances, the police in India till today could not outgrow the role assigned to them more than a hundred years ago. Myriads of statements have been made at all possible levels mentioning that the role of police has markedly changed after independence. It remains a long-felt and much lamented need that the law of the land clearly lays down what role the police should play in the decidedly changed socio-political life of the country. That will definitely remove considerable misgivings, clarify unwarranted expectations and strengthen the police machinery for the job it is meant to perform.

The importance of functional independence of the police has been well recognized even by the Supreme Court, illustrating that the statutory powers of the police to investigate into the circumstances of any alleged cognizable offence cannot be interfered with even by the judiciary. The legal position that emerges from this is that the police have complete functional independence in the investigation of cases and also enjoy considerable independence of action in matters of disposal of unlawful assemblies and maintenance of public order. The need of the time is that such independence is not only preserved but enhanced to make the police force more effective and responsible.

This definitely brings one to examine the question of control over the police. As per the Police Act 1861, (Section 4) the ultimate responsibility for the maintenance of law and order lies with the District Magistrate. Why then is the question raised about the police being responsible or accountable to anybody else than the District Magistrate? The duties of the police under the statutory law and the role of police as envisaged in the popular and welfare democracy to which we are wedded, come in the way of police becoming accountable to District Magistrate. The magisterial brake on the police, thought necessary over a century ago, should go if the concept of police accountability in a democratic society is really to gain ground or stand the test of practical validity.

The considerations that arise when this issue of police accountability is viewed as a practical political problem and not merely an academic exercise in political science, are also quite weighty and warrant serious thoughts. How does after all a democracy function? A feeling of being ultimately responsible to the State Legislature or Parliament runs through the entire fabric of public services. So it is said that the primary or the pivotal force moving the wheels of administration in a democratic form of government comes from the political heads. Indeed the moral responsibility of a minister is very much a reality in a democratic form of government and in such a situation, a public service like the police cannot be unanswerable to the people's representatives. It is not for anything that day in and day out it is being asserted that the police should change their attitude and learn to grow in accordance with the aspirations of the people whom they serve.

The police has become specially vulnerable to interference because of the immense benefits reaped by the misuse of power. When power rather than authority becomes the hallmark of the police, mafia gangs, influential hoods and unscrupulous politicians collude with police to form an invincible corridor of brute power. The power-hungry politicians strive to use it for their own ends.

Similarly, the control by citizens has been cleverly substituted by civilian bureaucrats. The police, for years, have been lamenting and opposing this fact that they are constantly under the thumb of not only the politicians but also the civil servants. The reports of National Police Commission (1978-80) and the recent filing of Public Interest Litigation by two retired police officers are steps in this direction.

The answerability of the police is only to law, as exemplified in the concept of the police being 'Officers of law' is an idealistic proposition and as a theorem of administrative geometry appears unassailable. The immunity that is wanted for the police is, to put it bluntly, mainly against political contamination, because the other fetters imposed by Police Act, can be overcome in many ways. The point, however, remains as to whether it is really possible or even desirable to insulate the police completely against all outside influence—call it by any name—interference or direction.

There is an element of positive dislike and distrust in the general feelings of the public towards a policeman. Maligned, hated, discredited—that has become the lot of policemen in India. Even a judge describes them as, "the biggest organised gang of criminals." They are being 'used' by some, 'abused' by others and 'ignored' by the vast majority. A policeman is expected to behave with impeccable courtesy with those who want to smash his head or knock out his teeth with a small gesture of political exuberance; he is supposed to protect the criminals who become political bosses and are provided X, Y or Z category securities; he is supposed to enforce laws some of which are already out-dated and are even against the Constitution, he is supposed to be accountable not only to law, people and his organisation but to almost everything and everybody.

Name a problem and you will probably find that somewhere in the country there is a policeman assigned to help solve it. In the last few decades insurgency, terrorism and communal riots have made the job even more difficult for a policeman. Under such trying circumstances, the demands made on the policemen by the public, the police organisation and the judiciary are quite conflicting to each other. When a situation goes out of hand, the policeman is asked to control it by hook or by 'danda'. The moment situation is brought under control, even though at a great cost of loss to police life, there is immediate talk of judicial enquiries and commissions. If the police acts, it is condemned for excesses, if it does not act, it is condemned for inaction. It is really a tight-rope walking for the police in performing its duties most of which are not even codified. And the judges are also not sympathetic towards the plight of a policeman.

The recent spurt of judicial activism has further added new dimensions to the police accountability. In trying to please all its 'masters', the police in India could not satisfy any of them. It has been getting bashing from all of them. General impression of public about police has always been bad. Now the judiciary has also joined in whipping the police. How else one explains the comments of a distinguished judge calling the police as "the biggest organised gang of criminals."

The judges of the Apex Court have always acted keeping in view the larger interest of the country and its democratic values. As the conscience-keepers of the Constitution and the guardians of our Fundamental Rights their performance has definitely been commendable. However, it must be pointed out with all the humility at my command that some of them have started over playing the role assigned to them by our Constituent Assembly. Of late, it has been showing more determination to see that its writ runs through all the wings of the government. Many of the political bosses and police officers have learnt it the hard way and are cooling their heels in one jail or the other.

The politicisation of the police and the criminalisation of politics may carry this process of dominance by judiciary even further. To some extent, the judiciary is born great, some greatness has been acquired by it on the strength of the performance of some of its illustrious judges, but some of it has also been thrust on it by the failure of the other two organs of the State to do their duty properly. In the last few years or so our cabinet ministers have shown a deplorable tendency to shift the responsibility to the courts for matters which the government is too weak, too timid or too confused to decide for itself. We have lost all sense of propriety and are not only willing but eager to call upon the court to decide those questions which is the duty of the executive to decide firmly and courageously. While the essential function of the judiciary is to interpret law and not make it, of late it has been forced to do the latter.

The judiciary is being willy-nilly caught in a political web from which they do not know how to extricate themselves. Public interest litigations were originally meant to help the weak and the indigent who did not know where to go to seek judicial redress and how to go about it. This well-conceived practice has now been taken over by organised groups of various interests and has been trivialised into publicity gestures for pet causes ranging from banning autobiographies, supplying rations to terrorists held up in Hazratbal and determining the height of Sardar Sarovar dam to saving the Taj Mahal.

Judicial activism is laudable and definitely has a place in democracy. But certain lobbies, open or covert, are trying to divert it from its right course. Judges are, after all, human beings and not mere abstract embodiments of judicial fairplay, unmoved by high-voltage publicity. Judges trying the so-called 'VIP cases' are tending to become household names, and those accustomed to perform their onerous duties in a vacuum of anonymity may be dazzled by the glare of publicity that is suddenly focused on them. This may distort judicial perspective. Their primary function of quick dispensation of justice may get ignored, while judicial energy and resources are sapped by the VIP cases. The ends of justice is justice itself and that is getting affected. In other words, justice many a time is becoming untouchable. Justice for an ordinary man is almost impossible to get. Judicial activism doesn't mean anything to all those people who are waiting for the dispensation of justice. The same judiciary that has taken such a strict view (three months rigorous imprisonment and fine) for 'bottom-slapping' by Super Cop K.P.S. Gill is known for taking an outrageously lenient view when it comes to rape of a Bhanwari Devi or a Hamida.

Judicial activism is welcome. So is the activism in legislature and the activism in executive. There can be no place for somnolence in a society where so much waits to be done. But if activism in one area spills into activism in other branches of governance, unintended consequences could follow. It is one thing to say that CBI will complete the investigation in 15 days and file its report in the High Court. But, what about the quality of evidence collected when there is a race against time. When quick decisive results are demanded of police, the law enforcers in their eagerness to achieve the results may take law into their own hands.

Imagine the situation where the Apex Court blasts the Chief of Police in open court and directs him to arrest the accused who is absconding, and produce him in court within a month. Taking cue from the highest court, even the lower judiciary has started doing it. This is unheard of in Anglo-Saxon law, which we are following, where the court can try only those persons who are charged and arrayed before it. Doing justice is not the monopoly of the judiciary. The police cannot be merely presumed to be unjust or arbitrary in their actions.

Once again, it is the growing cynicism of judiciary vis-à-vis political class and the police which provides popular support for even some of the most audacious pronouncements by the courts of the land. And one pronouncement that must be taken note of is a High Court's order asking a Joint Director of the CBI not to report to his boss. There were other channels open to the court to ensure that there is no unnecessary interference, but the way it has acted is taking judicial activism too far. At stake here is the functioning of an important wing of police which has its own logical chain of hierarchy. And the logic of this hierarchical chain of command is that the fate of an investigation cannot depend only on the perception of an individual officer but should be subject to the proper scrutiny and application of mind by a series of officers. What is otherwise the guarantee that the angularities of a given officer will not result in a report biased for or against any person. This is not to argue that the courts have no business monitoring investigations. But it is surely presumptuous for the court to believe that it has the capability to do the actual investigations. A clear case of activism gone over board and defining absolutely new dimension of police accountability.

The court has every right to pull up a police officer for tardy investigation. It can pass strictures against him and order the department to conduct an enquiry into the lapses. But it cannot decide on which officer should conduct investigation or direct a junior official to bypass his senior. When junior officers do not answer to their seniors, how can the discipline and rule of law be maintained. The way courts have been asking police and CBI to complete investigation within 15 days or one month, isn't it again stretching judicial activism too far.

As a result of such arm-twisting of police by the judiciary, the investigative agencies are being put under so much pressure that they often make tall claims to please the judges, who these days are not prepared to accept anything less than chargesheet against celebrity accused, irrespective of whether there is evidence available or not. A most salutary principle of our judicial system has been that an accused should be deemed innocent until he is proved guilty in a court of law. In some of the recent cases, however, this principle seems to have been abandoned in favour of a new one that no man should be considered honest unless he is proved so in a court of law.

In the age of judicial activism, a degree of 'irritability', 'pomposity' and 'talkativeness' in several orders has been exhibited by the court. A holier-than-thou attitude of the judiciary is coming to the fore. The tendency to demean persons before the bench, ad hoc decisions to grant or withhold bail, and the attitude of the judiciary when it comes to contempt of court are three areas where judicial discretion must walk hand in hand with judicial restraint. How can a judge pull up the investigating agency for not arresting an accused, especially in anti-corruption cases where the accused cannot afford to run away from justice. In such cases the timing and need of arrest has to be decided by the investigator and not by the judge, unless the accused is put up for trial. The judiciary needs to guard against judicial expansionism and stick to its own role.

Judges, like all others in the society, have their own proclivities and social biases. It will definitely be dangerous if they usurp the powers of other wings of the government without themselves being accountable to anybody. Has any judge been ever pulled up for inordinate delays in disposal of cases, improper appreciation of legal issues, overpromptness in issuing stay orders and undue haste in granting bail to those accused of heinous crimes?

Irrelevant, archaic, often non-sensical, a time-consuming edifice that revels in red tape, that is the Indian legal system in nutshell. If it sounds too harsh, consider these statistics. About two-thirds of our laws have not been used in Independent India. About 10 per cent of them can be scrapped right away. And most of the 40 per cent in use currently have so many obsolete and conflicting provisions that they serve more as instruments of harassment than effective means of justice. Most of them cater to a colonial and feudal socio-economic milieu. Law is for the society. So the law should change as and when society changes, changes in society will not be determined by law. In the past century and a half the socio-economic framework of the country has undergone radical changes, but our legal system has failed to keep pace with it.

No doubt judicial activism is justified in more than one way. In a country where everybody's business is nobody's business, suddenly there is someone asking questions and punishing the delinquent. If the gavel of courtly order, which has virtually turned into a sledgehammer strikes at irresponsible officers, corrupt politicians and power-drunk policemen, it will remain a welcome step. However, any attempt on the part of the judiciary to take over the supervening role in the administration of the country can land us in disaster. Judicial despotism is not only unreasonable but also irrational. Too much of judicial activism could erode the credibility of courts, imperil the rule of law and lead to lawlessness.

In the last about 20 years, the Indian Police has seen the full spectrum of the judiciary from the 'committed judiciary' to the 'activist judiciary'. No rational thinker wants to return to the days when judges blindly enforced laws. Yet nor does anyone desire a day when a judge will make laws. Laws and institutions, like clocks, must occasionally be cleaned and wound up, and set to true time. True time, indeed. Because the judges shouldn't reflect weather of the day, but wisdom of the ages.

The judges cannot run the country? I hope they are not aiming to do so; all they, especially the higher judiciary, seem to be saying is, "you leaders, please stop robbing the country and start running it". All over the country debates are being stoked on the issue of judicial activism. Some interested parties may raise dust so that the judges who are attempting to apply these modest correctives get discredited and the culprits run off in the confusion. Far from falling prey to the 'debates' we should use the opportunity offered by courts and actively assist them in reversing the breakdown of norms and institutions. Perhaps Delhi Riot cases, St. Kitts, Hawala, Gwala, the cases on protection of environment, Housing Scam could never have reached any logical end but for judicial activism. In other words, probing corruption in high places could not have been possible in the light of executive failure and the legislative inadequacies; (remember the role and record of the two Joint Parliamentary Committees) in dealing with such cases, had the judiciary not used the whip lash.

The judiciary definitely has a positive role to play in safeguarding the constitution. But the cardinal principle is that it must function within its own domain and not encroach into other's spheres. The functional independence of the police in our country, as laid down in the law, is largely satisfactory even though the actual practice differs from the principle considerably. In a country where tradition dies hard, illiteracy is still stalking and the bulk of the 'custodians of law' or 'guardians of peace' are steeped in both, the concept of making them all 'officers of law' in the absolute sense may well be laudable but a luxury that we can perhaps ill afford in actual practice at the present time.

What is actually needed is a balanced approach and to devise a mechanism that should ensure that the police discharge their statutory responsibilities and meet the aspirations of the general public without any bias. The openness of public enquiries, a bit of transparency in the working, the confidence of the police department to expose itself for external scrutiny are factors that build trust amongst the people and begin the process of making the police accountable. Above all, it must be realised that for this to happen the police chiefs need to have operational freedom and the strength and courage to tackle the external interferences. The police cannot be controlled by external agencies. The departmental heads have to be given the powers and mandate to professionalise their organisations and then be held accountable for the actions of their subordinates. On the other hand, the police leadership must seek ways of opening up and initiate bold imaginative actions that alone can save the organisation and themselves; for organisations never die due to outside factors and influences, but due to decay from within.

The judiciary admittedly has a positive role to play in safeguarding the constitution. But the traditional principle that it must function within its own domain and not encroach into others' areas, the [illegible] the police [illegible] as laid down in the law, is largely sacrosanct even though the [illegible] practice [illegible] where [illegible] of the questions of law or procedure [illegible] with the concept of making them [illegible] of law in the [illegible] but a [illegible] that we can perhaps afford [illegible] at the present time.

When a [illegible] in a [illegible] expression and the [illegible] enquiries [illegible] the conduct of the police department [illegible]

22

JUSTICE ON TRIAL

K. Mahesh

I hold Indian Judiciary in great esteem, particularly the apex judiciary which is really the finest of the three pillars of our Constitution and has done a great pride to the constitutional system of India. But to compliment is not to become complacent and it is with this spirit of constructive criticism that I address the present topic.

The Supreme Court has introduced the element of requirement of fairness in administrative matters, i.e., the administrative decisions must be reasonable, just and fair. An important case in this connection is the Menaka Gandhi case. However, we have to keep in mind that judges are not elected by people and they are not accountable to the common man, the way politicians are. Politicians have to go to the public every five years and more often than not even sooner than five years. Bureaucrats are accountable to their ministers, the legislature, the courts and other watchdog bodies like the C.V.C. and the C.B.I. Judiciary correctly says that there should not be any administrative arbitrariness. But what are the safeguards against judicial arbitrariness? If lower courts go wrong one can approach the High Court and Supreme Court. But heavens forbid if Supreme Court goes wrong as to err is but human, what is the way out?

The most alarming judgement was one delivered during the emergency which stated that an ordinary citizen would not have a fundamental right to life. It is heartening to note that this was subsequently denounced and disowned by the judges themselves.

The Supreme Court entertained an application in Thapar's case granting bail when approached directly from a magistrate's order of refusal. That case is known as "midnight case" which evoked good deal of public concern.

Rajan Pillai was denied freedom of movement by a magistrate in Delhi; simultaneously a magistrate in Madras granted bail to Sushil Sharma of the Tandoor Murder Case. Recently the Supreme Court directed the PM to enact a common civil code. This was a case of clear tresspass in the province of Parliament.

The Supreme Court delivered a judgement on increasing the retirement age of judges in the subordinate court and also laid down the terms and conditions of their service. This is in the domain of legislation.

Delhi High Court had quashed the Bofors FIR in one of the PILs filed by Harvinder Singh Chowdhary. This decision was fortunately overturned in an appeal by the Supreme Court (Janata Dal vs. H.S. Chowdhary AIR 1993 SC 892), leading to the ongoing investigation about the payoffs and possible connections with the Hawala Case.

The court's contempt jurisprudence is messy and ad hoc. The court pulled up one of its lawyers for the inadvertent filing of misleading drafts; and dealt with Punjab officials for their savage violation of the rule of law severely. Yet, its decision in the Vasudevan case, imprisoning a civil servant both astonished and sent shudders down the back of bureaucracy who have in other cases also been put on notice that they will be personally liable for gross contempts and violation of the rule of law. Bombay lawyers who were virtually browbeating the then Chief Justice Bhattacharya to resign were warned to show restraint. Yet, in the Sariska case, the court did no more than issue a warning to a person who had intimidated senior counsel physically and not even bothered to turn up to Supreme Court hearings when mandated to do so. In 1970, the Marxist leader E.M.S. Namboodripad was fined by Supreme Court for what it described as scandalising the judges by alleging that they were "biased against the working class". And, in 1988, the then Union Law Minister P. Shivshankar faced contempt proceedings for alleging "antisocial elements, FERA violators, bride burners and hordes of reactionaries have found their heaven in the Supreme Court." But a bench headed by Justice Sabyasachi Mukherji sidestepping the Namboodripad verdict, exonerated Shivshankar. There is a need to adopt some self-imposed limitation in their contempt jurisdiction. The strongest justification for relaxing contempt laws came as early as 1941 when United States Supreme Court ruled in Bridges vs State of California that scandalising the court could not be ground for contempt. Justice Hugo Black, a champion of individual rights, observed: "The assumption that respect for the judiciary can be won by shielding judges from published criticism wrongly appraises the character of American public opinion. An enforced silence however limited solely in the name of preserving the dignity of the bench would probably engender resentment, suspicion and contempt much more than it would enhance respect."

In 1993, the Supreme Court delivered a majority judgement which denied the executive a say in the matter of appointment of Supreme Court/High Court judges and conferred this power exclusively on the judiciary. The appointment of judges in the apex court should not be left to the judiciary or to the executive alone as it is not a fool-proof, method. We must evolve a collective process with wider consultative access to judges, lawyers, politicians and the public.

None can disagree with Jerome Frank, a great American judge, whose work *Courts on Trial* is a classic, "I am unable to conceive that in democracy, it can ever be unwise to acquaint the public with the truth about the workings of any branch of Government. It is wholly undemocratic to treat the public as children who are unable to accept the inescapable shortcomings of manmade institutions . . . . The best way to bring about the elimination of those shortcomings of our judicial system which are capable of being eliminated is to have all our citizens informed as to how that system now functions. It is a mistake, therefore, to try to establish and maintain through ignorance, public esteem for our courts."

To say that there is no corruption at all in judiciary particularly at the lower level is being blind to the existing ground realities.

Former Chief Justice Waren Burger noted, "A sense of confidence in the courts is essential to maintain the fabric of order, liberty for free people and three things could destroy that confidence and do incalculable damage to society:

(i) That people come to believe that inefficiency and delay will drain even a just judgement of its values.

(ii) That people who have long been exploited in the smaller transactions in daily life come to believe that courts cannot vindicate their legal rights from fraud and overreaching.

(iii) That people come to believe the law in the larger sense cannot fulfil its primary function to protect them and their families in their homes, at their work and on the public streets".

One of the most remarkable judges of the American Supreme Court, Justice Holmes who was a judge of the American Supreme Court for more than 30 years said, "Long time back I realized that I may be justice of the Supreme Court but I am not a demi - god that was the starting point of my wisdom."

May be Indian judges can serve the nation with the same sense of purpose and humility.

Those who advocate justice must do justice. Judges are the instrument but justice is the end. May I quote Mr. Justice J.S. Verma, the former Chief Justice of Supreme Court: "The Judges have to accept the maxim, be you ever so high, the law is above you applies to them as well."

INDEX